RAND

Dire Demographics

Population Trends in the Russian Federation

Julie DaVanzo
Clifford Grammich

Supported by the
William and Flora Hewlett Foundation
David and Lucile Packard Foundation
Rockefeller Foundation

POPULATION MATTERS
A RAND Program of Policy-Relevant Research Communication

The research described in this report was supported by the William and Flora Hewlett Foundation, the David and Lucile Packard Foundation, and the Rockefeller Foundation.

Library of Congress Cataloging-in-Publication Data

DaVanzo, Julie.
Dire demographics : population trends in the Russian Federation / Julie DaVanzo, Clifford Grammich.
p. cm.
"MR-1273."
Includes bibliographical references.
ISBN 0-8330-2930-4
1. Russia (Federation)—Population—Statistics. 2. Demographic transition—Russia (Federation) 3. Russia (Federation)—Social conditions—1991– I. Grammich, Clifford, 1943– II. Title.

HB3608.2.A3 D38 2001
304.6'0947—dc21

2001034955

Published 2001 by RAND
1700 Main Street, P.O. Box 2138, Santa Monica, CA 90407-2138
1200 South Hayes Street, Arlington, VA 22202-5050
201 North Craig Street, Suite 102, Pittsburgh, PA 15213
RAND URL: http://www.rand.org/
To order RAND documents or to obtain additional information, contact Distribution Services: Telephone: (310) 451-7002;
Fax: (310) 451-6915; Email: order@rand.org

PREFACE

Since the fall of the Soviet Union, the demographics of the Russian Federation have revealed several adverse trends. Although thought to be recent, many of these trends actually continue the rocky demographic history that characterized the Soviet Union. These demographic variables indicate substantial challenges confronting both policymakers within the Russian Federation and members of the international community concerned about Russia. This report reviews the major demographic trends that are currently affecting Russian social welfare and that will shape options for Russian policymakers in future years.

This report grew out of a conference on "Russia's Demographic Crisis in Comparative Perspective," held in 1995 at RAND with researchers from Russia's Center for Demography and Human Economy, part of the Russian Academy of Sciences. In 1996, RAND issued conference proceedings that included the major papers delivered at the conference (DaVanzo, 1996). In 1997, we published an issue paper based on the conference proceedings that used updated statistics where available (DaVanzo and Adamson, 1997). For this report, we have again updated information based on the latest available statistics. We have also updated and expanded our interpretations of these statistics and their implications.

This research has been presented to the U.S. State Department Bureau of Intelligence and Research, the Winter Colloquium of the Morrison Institute for Population and Resource Studies at Stanford University, the board of directors for the Center for Russia and Eurasia at RAND, and the RAND board of trustees.

This report, which should be of interest to all persons who are concerned about the policy implications of demographic issues in Russia, was prepared for the *Population Matters* project within the RAND Labor and Population Program. The primary focus of *Population Matters* is synthesizing and communicating the findings and implications of existing research in ways that policy analysts and others will find accessible.

The *Population Matters* project is funded by grants from the William and Flora Hewlett Foundation, the David and Lucile Packard Foundation, and the Rockefeller Foundation. For a complete list of *Population Matters* publications, please see the inside back cover of this report. For further information on the *Population Matters* project, visit the project Web site at http://www.rand.org/popmatters.

CONTENTS

Preface iii

Figures vii

Tables ix

Summary xi

Acknowledgments xvii

Chapter One

RUSSIAN DEMOGRAPHY AND ITS IMPLICATIONS 1
Russian Demographic Trends in the 1990s 1
Policy Issues Arising from Demographic Trends 5

Chapter Two

POPULATION CHANGE IN RUSSIA 9
Population Loss in the 1990s 9
Immigration 13

Chapter Three

FERTILITY IN RUSSIA 21
Trends in Fertility 21
Abortion and Contraception 25
History of Abortion and Contraception in Russia 28
Recent Declines in Abortion 31
The Role of Contraception in Reducing Abortion 32
Reaction Against Contraception and Abortion 35
Prospects for Future Fertility and Population Growth . . 36

Chapter Four

CAUSES AND IMPLICATIONS OF RUSSIAN MORTALITY . 37
Russian Population Losses and Declining Life Expectancy 37
Increasing Mortality for Working-Age Males 40
Changing Causes of Working-Age Male Mortality 43
Health Care in Russia 48
Resurgence of Russian Tuberculosis 51
The Growth of HIV/AIDS in Russia 55
Conclusion 56
Explanations for Recent Trends in Russian Working-Age Mortality 57
Environment 57
Alcohol 58
Social and Economic Change 61

Chapter Five

DEMOGRAPHIC HISTORY, AGE STRUCTURE, AND FUTURE POLICY ISSUES 63
Age and Sex Structure of the Russian Population 63
Policy Implications of the Current Population Age Structure 66
Elderly Population 66
Working-Age Population 68
Military-Age Population 69
Youth Population 71
Dependency Ratios 71

Chapter Six

WHAT CAN BE DONE TO ADDRESS DEMOGRAPHIC POLICY ISSUES IN RUSSIA? 75
Health Care Education 75
Health Care System and Financing 77
Other Government Health Initiatives 79
Long-Term Issues 81

BIBLIOGRAPHY 85

FIGURES

1.1. Russian Concern About the Demographic Situation . . 2
1.2. Population Density (Persons per Square Kilometer) by Region, 1998 6
2.1. Population Change by Region, 1989–98 10
2.2. Net Domestic Migration per 10,000 Population by Region, 1997 11
2.3. Births and Deaths in Russia, 1959–99 12
2.4. Natural Population Change Per 1,000 Population by Region, 1997 13
2.5. Natural Population Growth and Net Immigration in Russia, 1959–98 14
2.6. Net Immigration by Ethnicity between Russia and Other Former Soviet Republics 16
2.7. Net International Immigration per 10,000 Population by Region, 1997 17
3.1. Total Fertility Rate in Russia and Six Western Nations 22
3.2. Total Fertility Rate in Russia, Hungary, and Poland . . . 25
3.3. Crude Birth Rate (Births per 1,000 Population) by Region, 1997 26
3.4. Abortion Rates in Selected Countries, 1995–96 27
3.5. Russian Abortion Rates and Ratios, 1970–97 31
3.6. Abortion and Contraceptive Use in Russia, 1988–97 . . 33
4.1. Trends in Russian and U.S. Life Expectancy by Sex, 1926–99 39
4.2. Russian Life Expectancy by Region, 1997 40

4.3. Mortality Increases by Age and Sex and Their Contribution to Changes in Life Expectancy by Sex, 1990–94 41
4.4. Mortality by Sex for Russians Aged 15–64, 1965–97 . . . 42
4.5. Contribution of Different Causes of Death to Changes in Russian Male Life Expectancy, 1984–96 45
4.6. Rates of Death by Leading Causes for Males Aged 15–64 in Russia and the United States, 1994–95 47
4.7. Tuberculosis Rates in Russia and Some Other Nations and Regions 52
4.8. Russian Rates of Death from Tuberculosis and All Other Causes, 1965–97 53
4.9. Total Alcohol Consumption and Russian Male Life Expectancy, 1984–93 59
4.10. Alcohol Consumption and Life Expectancy for Russian Males, 1992–98 60
5.1. Typical Population Pyramid 64
5.2. Russian Population "Pyramid" 65
5.3. Russian Dependency Ratios, 1990–2020 72
5.4. Pension-Age Dependency Ratio by Region, 1998 73
6.1. Infant Mortality Rate (Infant Deaths per 1,000 Live Births) by Region, 1997 80

TABLES

1.1. Estimated and Projected Populations for 15 Most Populous Nations, 2000, 2010, and 2040 4

SUMMARY

In the past decade, the Russian Federation has experienced many seemingly unfavorable demographic trends, the two most significant of which are a declining number of births and a rising number of deaths. These trends are likely to continue for some time. Some analysts fear that the Russian population, currently at about 145 million, could decline to less than 100 million. This demographic decline raises several issues for Russia, including the need for health care improvements; the challenges posed by a declining working-age population to support a growing elderly population; and still other issues affecting Russia's ability to reform its economy, government, and society. This report examines trends in overall population size, fertility rates, and mortality rates and issues in health care, elderly support, and national security arising from these trends.

Since 1992, the population of Russia has declined by three million. The annual number of Russian births fell by 1.3 million between 1987 and 1999, while the annual number of Russian deaths increased by 500,000. Net immigration has prevented Russian population losses from being even greater, with many ethnic Russians migrating to Russia from borderlands formerly in the Soviet Union. The most recent statistics, however, indicate that this ethnic Russian immigration is declining and, as a result, it is unlikely to be an important source of population stabilization in the future. There is also public resistance to immigration and concerns about the security risks created by immigration of nonethnic Russians. If Russian immigration cannot be increased, then the only other alternatives for population stability are to increase birth rates or to reduce death rates.

Russian fertility rates fell throughout the 20th century. A century ago, Russian women bore, on average, more than seven children in a lifetime; today, this average is just over one. Declining fertility rates are not unique to Russia. Since the 1950s, fertility rates have fallen throughout Europe and North America and are now below replacement level (about 2.1 children per woman) in a number of nations. Soviet officials periodically attempted to boost fertility with pronatalist incentives, but, as has happened in every other nation instituting such incentives, these failed to boost fertility significantly for an extended period of time. The increase in fertility arising from the most recent pronatalist effort in the 1980s appears to have affected the timing of births more than their ultimate number.

The economic conditions of the 1990s appear to have had their own effect on Russian fertility rates. Whereas the Russian fertility rate in the early 1990s was comparable to that of France and the United Kingdom, and just below that of the United States, today it is among the lowest in the world. Birth rates do not decline or remain low solely because of economic troubles, however. Both Spain and Italy have fertility rates as low as that for Russia despite having seen great economic improvements in recent decades. Within Eastern Europe, economic recovery in nations such as Hungary and Poland has not reversed fertility rate declines.

Accompanying the low fertility rate in Russia is one of the highest abortion rates in the world. Some Russian women have had ten or more abortions in their lifetimes; more than three in four Russian women who have ever been pregnant have had an abortion. Currently about 70 percent of Russian pregnancies end in abortion. The substantial health problems caused by high rates of abortion, including secondary sterility and health complications, and the resulting stress on the health system have led to recent efforts to increase contraceptive use. Prior to the 1990s, abortion was the main means of fertility regulation used by Russian women, but wider availability of modern means of contraception has led to a decline in abortion rates in recent years.

In the shorter term, population problems indicated by high mortality levels may be more amenable to immediate policy initiatives. As the Soviet health system helped bring infectious and communicable diseases under control, Russian life expectancy at birth increased rapidly and nearly matched that of the United States in the mid-1960s. Since then, however, little progress has been made in Russia against "civilization" diseases, i.e., the causes of death, such as neoplasms and cardiovascular diseases, more prevalent in advanced societies. This is particularly apparent in the climbing death rates for working-age males. In recent years, deaths to working-age males from circulatory diseases and from external causes—particularly accidents, poisoning, or violence that accompany high levels of alcohol consumption typical of Russia—have had the greatest adverse effect on Russian male life expectancy, which is lower now than it was in the mid-1960s.

Because of its emphasis on specialized acute curative care over general preventive care, the Russian health system cannot effectively address the problems it currently faces. Furthermore, given its deterioration in recent years, it is falling behind against diseases it had largely brought under control. Tuberculosis death rates, for example, are now at their highest levels in nearly 30 years. Other ominous problems loom; intravenous drug use in particular has led to a rapidly growing HIV/AIDS problem.

In addition to a deteriorating health care system, other problems affect Russian health and mortality, including a polluted environment, high rates of alcohol and tobacco consumption, and social and economic change. The Soviets treated the Russian environment recklessly for decades, and industrial pollution remains much higher than that prevalent in the European Economic Community. While such extreme conditions can adversely affect public health, they cannot explain the concentration of health problems among working-age males or the recent sharp fluctuations in overall mortality rates. Russian alcohol consumption, which is higher among males than females, has been strongly correlated with working-age male mortality in recent years. Whenever alcohol consumption declined during the past two decades (e.g., during the antialcohol campaign of the mid-1980s), male life expectancy increased. Social and economic change have also contributed to deteriorating health and increasing mortality, particularly through an increase in cardiovascular diseases related to stress after the breakup of the Soviet Union.

The unique demographic history and conditions of Russia have given it a unique age structure. In coming years, Russia can expect growth in its elderly population but shrinkage in its working-age and youth populations. Population aging will present more challenges to a health system already facing myriad other problems. The government has few resources to strengthen the safety net for the elderly, and the elderly have few resources of their own on which they can draw. Declining cohorts at younger ages also pose special problems. The number of Russians of military age will soon decline sharply. Many European states with declining populations have been able to develop technologically sophisticated and capital-intensive forces to maintain their military strength, but it is unclear whether such a course is open to Russia. If Russia cannot pursue force modernization to compensate for its declining numbers of military-age youths, it may be forced to rely on weapons of mass destruction, including nuclear weapons, for its security. Fluctuations in youth populations will also affect planning for health and educational services.

What can be done to address policy issues arising from demographic trends in Russia? In the short term, improvements to the health care system might be most beneficial. Continuing improvements in contraceptive access can help Russian women to lead more stable and healthy reproductive lives. Broader public health education, similar to that undertaken in the United States, can help improve Russian health behaviors. Neighboring nations can also offer Russia many lessons both in health education and in restructuring its health system. Judicious spending of additional health care funds, particularly if taking into account regional variation in health care problems, also might yield immediate benefits.

Many long-term demographic problems may prove intractable without substantial economic improvement. Russia has tried to boost its fertility rate and population with pronatalist incentives, but these were not effective for long, and Russia cannot now afford to fund such incentives at a level that could have a perceptible effect on fertility rates. Immigration can, theoretically, help stabilize a declining population, but the Russian public is not likely to tolerate the high levels of immigration needed to offset large natural population losses. Because of its recently improving economy and current trends resulting from its unique population age structure (particularly a respite before resumption of growth in its elderly population), Russia does have a window of opportunity to address its demographic issues and their implications. In doing so, Russia may find it better to focus more on qualitative indicators, such as the health and welfare of its current population, rather than on quantitative indicators, such as the overall size of its population, in improving its demographic health.

ACKNOWLEDGMENTS

The authors gratefully acknowledge the many helpful comments on previous drafts that came from formal and informal reviews by Jeremy Azrael, Cynthia Buckley, Daniel Goldberg, Ward Kingkade, D. J. Peterson, and Sergei Zakharov. We also acknowledge the help Irina Sharkova and Alexei Krindatch gave us by providing information about software used to make the maps in this work. We appreciate the editorial guidance of Steve Baeck and Phyllis Gilmore and the assistance that Sandy Petitjean, Bruce Cheeks, and Rod Sato provided with the figures in this report.

Chapter One

RUSSIAN DEMOGRAPHY AND ITS IMPLICATIONS

RUSSIAN DEMOGRAPHIC TRENDS IN THE 1990s

Throughout the 1990s, Russia has experienced many seemingly unfavorable demographic trends. The number, depth, and interaction of these trends have led many to suggest that Russia is experiencing a demographic "crisis." The fall in the number of Russian births, coupled with a rise in the number of deaths, has caused concern among many Russians (Figure 1.1).

When the number of deaths first exceeded the number of births shortly after the fall of the Soviet Union, many popular media analyses suggested the need "to save Russia from depopulation."[1] Communists, self-proclaimed patriots, and devout churchgoers periodically implore the Duma to address the dire demographics of Russia by providing benefits to couples rearing children, limiting contraceptive access, restricting abortion rights, or even permitting polygamy (Zakharov, 1999a; Klomegah, 2001). Many persons blame the "neoliberal" economic policies instituted by Russia after the fall of the Soviet Union for the demographic "crisis," with some labeling its results as "genocide."[2]

---

[1] See Zakharov and Ivanova (1996) for discussion of public reaction to demographic trends.

[2] For discussion of elite Russian opinion on demographic conditions, see Field (2000). One of the five principal accusations that the Russian Duma made in an ill-fated attempt to remove Boris Yeltsin from office in the spring of 1999 was that he had presided over the "genocide" of the Russian people (Zakharov, 1999c).

RAND *MR1273-1.1*

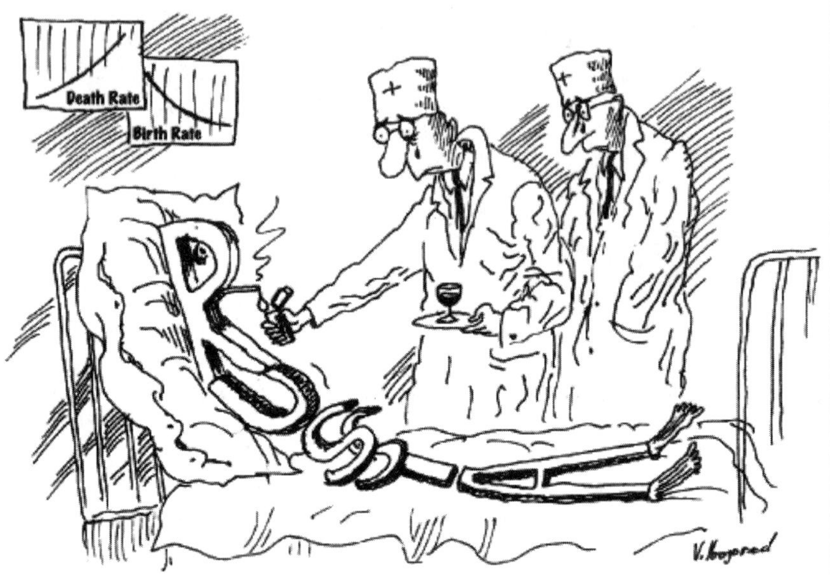

Doctors' best efforts can't curb Russia's population decline

SOURCE: Reprinted with permission from Moscow *Times*, January 27, 2000. Artist V. Bogorod.

Figure 1.1—Russian Concern About the Demographic Situation

The more rapid population growth of non-Russian ethnic groups in the federation during recent years has underscored the demographic decline of ethnic Russians. Among the 23 largest ethnic groups in Russia, only 10 have had smaller rates of recent growth than ethnic Russians, and many of these are groups such as Germans, Jews, and Ukrainians that have had high rates of emigration in recent years (RF Goskomstat, 1999a).[3]

---

[3]In personal correspondence, Cynthia Buckley (2000) indicates that ethnic nationalism has clouded Russian perceptions of demographic issues for decades. Analyses of the early 1970s, for example, such as that by Zaslavskaia and Kalmyk (1972) noting that several rural Soviet villages were not demographically viable in the long term, were attacked as anti-Russian and efforts to destroy the Russian soul by destroying the rural village. Anti-Semitic sentiments also on occasion clouded popular judgment of demographic studies and analyses.

The postponement for at least three years of the national census scheduled for 1999, which would have been the first complete census in the post-Soviet era, led to some speculation that the situation is so severe the Russian government does not want its full extent to be known (Karush, 1999).[4] Russian President Vladimir Putin has not proposed formal or explicit government measures to deal with demographic problems, but he has offered his own diagnosis of them. In his State of the Nation Address to the Duma in July 2000, he said, "For many people, it is difficult to bring up children, to secure for their parents the conditions for a dignified old age. It is difficult to live. Year by year, we, the citizens of Russia, are getting fewer and fewer. . . . We face the threat of becoming a senile nation" (Reuters, 2000b). Putin's cabinet reiterated its intentions to develop a plan to improve Russia's health and increase its birth rate and immigration (Karush, 2001).

Russians themselves are aware of the declining birth rate and the rising death rate. Many blame alcohol and tobacco consumption for poor Russian health, as seen in the *Moscow Times* cartoon reproduced in Figure 1.1. Other popular explanations for recent population losses include stress and dislocations resulting from the fall of communism, the collapse of the Soviet-era health care system, and "ecocide," i.e., the poisoning of the air, land, and water during Soviet

---

[4] A more likely and less alarming reason for the postponement of the census is the present inability of the Russian government to conduct it. In personal correspondence, Sergei Zakharov (2000a) indicates that "the experience of previous censuses of the USSR [is] of no use. The previous censuses were taken in conditions of a totalitarian state based on the planned economy and included a rather limited list of questions which is unsatisfactory." The Soviet government could compel, in a way the Russian Federation cannot, both compliance with the census and the participation of more than one million interviewers from the ranks of teachers, physicians, faculty and students of universities, and others. Furthermore, the Russian Federation has few persons skilled enough to organize and conduct a census and is slowly adopting the technology, primarily based on a network of personal computers rather than centralized mainframe machines, needed to tabulate a modern census. Finally, the Russian Ministry of Justice contends that laws on the conduct of the census contradict the constitution of the Russian Federation, allowing surveys only with the voluntary agreement of participants. Nevertheless, Russia is making progress toward its goal of conducting a census in October 2002. The State Statistics Committee has been working with the Justice Ministry toward an acceptable legal formulation enabling it to submit a draft census law to the Duma, stipulating that it is permissible to gather information on individuals for abstract, or statistical, rather than personal purposes (Vedomosti, 2001). The Committee recently conducted a trial census in select areas (Yablokova, 2000b).

times (Yablokova, 2000a). We explore the validity of these explanations in Chapters Three and Four of this report.

The decreasing population of Russia, combined with continued rapid growth in several large developing countries, means that Russia is increasingly less prominent among the most populous nations of the world. For most of the past half century, the USSR was the third most populous country in the world, and Russia by itself would have comprised the fourth most populous nation, surpassed only by China, India, and the United States. In 2000, Russia had the sixth largest population in the world, behind that of Indonesia and Brazil, as well as China, India, and the United States (Table 1.1). At its projected rate of population loss, by 2010 Russia is expected to be only the ninth most populous nation in the world, as Pakistan, Bangladesh, and Nigeria are all projected to surpass it. Long-term projections are even more foreboding for the standing of Russia; by

Table 1.1

Estimated and Projected Populations for 15 Most Populous Nations, 2000, 2010, and 2040

2000			2010			2040		
Rk	Country	Pop	Rk	Country	Pop	Rk	Country	Pop
1	China	1,262	1	China	1,359	1	India	1,540
2	India	1,014	2	India	1,168	2	China	1,492
3	USA	281	3	USA	300	3	USA	378
4	Indonesia	225	4	Indonesia	260	4	Indonesia	329
5	Brazil	173	5	Brazil	187	5	Nigeria	261
6	**Russia**	**145**	6	Pakistan	171	6	Pakistan	249
7	Pakistan	142	7	Nigeria	156	7	Brazil	207
8	Bangladesh	129	8	Bangladesh	150	8	Bangladesh	197
9	Japan	127	**9**	**Russia**	**142**	9	Ethiopia	156
10	Nigeria	123	10	Japan	127	10	Congo	149
11	Mexico	100	11	Mexico	115	11	Mexico	148
12	Germany	83	12	Phillipines	98	12	Phillipines	143
13	Phillipines	81	13	Vietnam	90	**13**	**Russia**	**127**
14	Vietnam	79	14	Germany	85	14	Vietnam	116
15	Egypt	68	15	Ethiopia	82	15	Japan	109

SOURCE: U.S. Census Bureau (2000).
NOTES: Rk = rank. Pop = population (in millions).

2040, current long-term projections show Ethiopia, the Democratic Republic of the Congo, Mexico, and the Philippines all surpassing Russia in population. This has been difficult for some Russians to accept, given the legacy of Soviet gigantism and widespread and traditional views linking population size with military and economic strength.[5]

POLICY ISSUES ARISING FROM DEMOGRAPHIC TRENDS

Demographic trends in Russia are shaping policy options available to Russia and how the international community must deal with Russia. Some analysts hold that demographic conditions will prevent Russia from returning to the ranks of great powers in coming decades (Eberstadt, 1999). Demographic instability in Russia also may lead to political instability affecting both Russia and the international community.

Within Russia, demographic trends underscore the need for health care improvements; the problems the working-age population will face in supporting the growing elderly population; and still other issues affecting the ability of Russia to reform its economy, government, and society. The enormous size of Russia, comprising a territory about twice the size of the United States and straddling 11 time zones, means Russia also must deal with substantial regional variation in these trends and issues. Russia has, for example, a very uneven distribution of population. While population density in the western regions is similar to that of other nations in eastern Europe, large expanses of Siberia and the Far East have less than one person per square kilometer (Figure 1.2).

---

[5] Zakharov (1999b) notes that "pronatalist ideology was a long-established tradition [in the Soviet Union, which] regarded quantitative growth of human resources . . . as a specific means to escape economic problems as well as a source of continued expansion of military and geopolitical power."

RAND MR1273-1.2

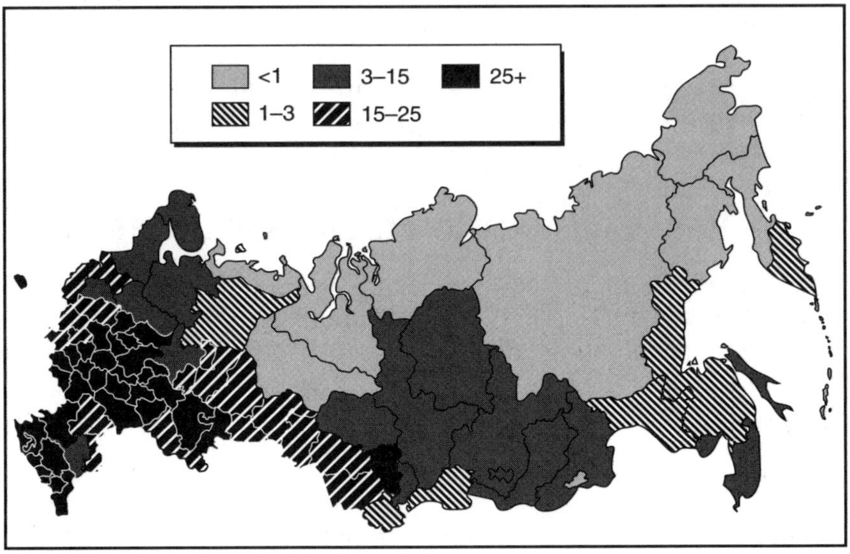

SOURCE: Pashintseva et al. (1998).

Figure 1.2—Population Density (Persons per Square Kilometer) by Region, 1998

Policymakers need to know the facts and understand the causes and consequences of demographic trends in Russia. Russia is certainly facing many worrying trends, but these vary in their severity, implications, and how much can be done to address them. As we will show in this report, many of these trends are not unique to the last decade in Russia. Some demographic trends in Russia are similar to those in many European countries. Others originated well before the fall of the Soviet Union and the advent of economic, political, and social reform, and will require time to change.

In this report, we examine these trends and discuss their underlying causes and policy implications. In Chapter Two, we examine trends in the overall population of Russia, including how migration to and from Russia has affected the size of the total population. In Chapter Three, we review declining fertility rates in Russia and their contribution to population decline and the trends in abortion and contraceptive use that underlie them. In Chapter Four, we examine increasing mortality rates and some of the explanations for high Russian death rates. In Chapter Five, we discuss the policy needs indicated by the current age distribution in Russia. We conclude in Chapter Six by noting some of the policy initiatives that might be undertaken to alleviate problems arising from Russian demographic conditions. Demographic trends pose great challenges to Russian policies on health care, elderly support, and national security. There are some measures that Russia can undertake now to meet these challenges, such as public health education or taking advantage of a demographic "window" available to prepare for an elderly population that will burgeon in size in coming years. Many aspects of these problems, however, may prove intractable to short-term policy initiatives; to address them will require more fundamental social and economic change.

Chapter Two

POPULATION CHANGE IN RUSSIA

POPULATION LOSS IN THE 1990s

Russia has lost population every year since 1992, when its resident population peaked at 148.4 million (Institut National d'Études Démographiques [INED], 2000). By late 2000, the Russian population had dropped to 145 million, a loss of more than 3 million in eight years, and Russian statisticians were predicting losses would continue for decades to come, including additional losses of 11 million persons by 2015 (*New York Times*, 2000; Karush, 2001).[1]

Population change has varied considerably by region in recent years. From 1989 to 1998 losses were heaviest in the North and Far East, while southern and southwestern regions, particularly the Volga and Caucasus regions, gained persons (Figure 2.1). These losses are attributable primarily to shifting patterns of domestic migration. Prior to the fall of the USSR, the Soviet government subsidized residence in the northern and eastern regions (Zayonchkovskaya, 1999a). Population growth from 1959 through 1989 was greatest in these areas (Pashintseva, Voronina, and Kazachenko, 1998).

---

[1] Most projections by other sources also show the Russian population will continue to decline in the next decade, but the range of these projected losses varies. For a range of Russian population forecasts for 2010, see Fedorov (1999), particularly p. 67, and Vishnevsky (1996). Some analysts fear that new crises, such as an AIDS epidemic, might accelerate Russian population losses, perhaps pushing the Russian population below 100 million; see, for example, Feshbach (2000). For an analysis of how population might shift by region in Russia, particularly from the north and east to the south and west, see Andreev, Scherbov, and Willekens (1998).

RAND *MR1273-2.1*

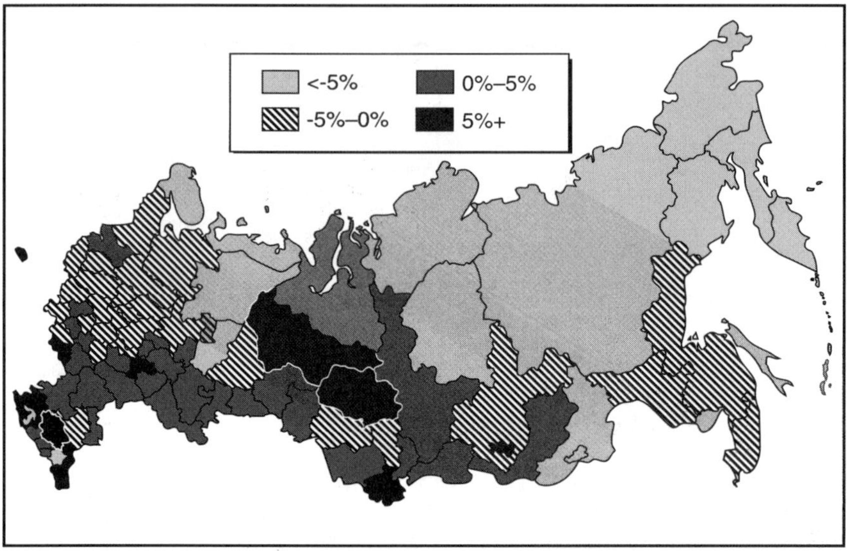

SOURCE: Pashintseva et al. (1998).

Figure 2.1—Population Change by Region, 1989–98

Following the elimination of these subsidies, many persons left these regions for the south and west. The most recent statistics on net domestic migration (or the excess of domestic migrants to a region over migrants from the region) show this movement continuing (Figure 2.2).

For Russia as a whole, a higher number of deaths than births has caused considerable population loss (Figure 2.3). The number of births dropped precipitously in the late 1980s and early 1990s, while the number of deaths has generally been increasing since 1960.[2] In each year since 1992, the number of deaths in Russia has exceeded the number of births. The number of deaths declined for a time in the mid-1990s but increased again late in the decade, following the economic crisis in 1998.

---

[2] All data that we cite, including that for the Soviet era, are for the territory that now comprises the Russian Federation.

RAND MR1273-2.2.

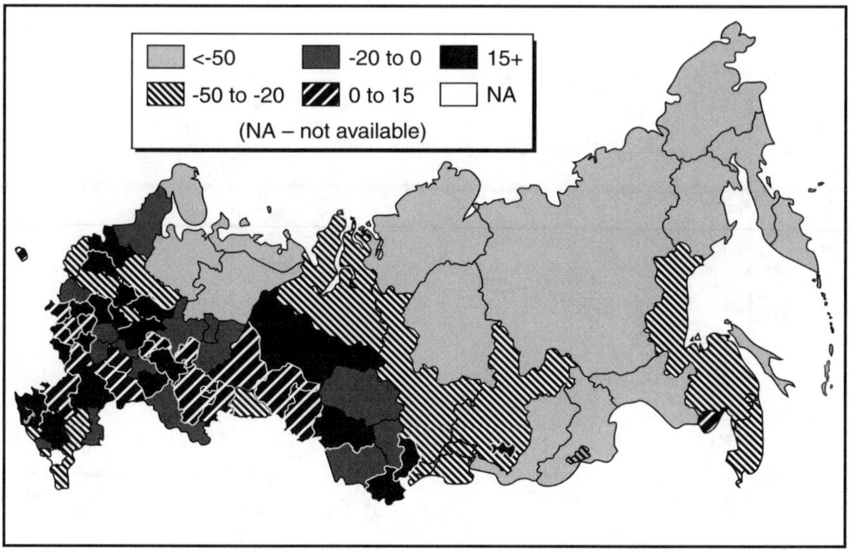

SOURCE: Pashintseva et al. (1998).

Figure 2.2—Net Domestic Migration per 10,000 Population by Region, 1997

The decline in Russian births bears more responsibility than the increase in the number of deaths for recent Russian population losses. Between 1987 and 1999, for example, the annual number of Russian births declined by 1.3 million, while the annual number of Russian deaths increased by only 500,000.

From 1992 through 1999, the cumulative number of deaths exceeded the number of births by nearly six million. There are a few other nations where the number of deaths has exceeded the number of births in recent years, but only in Bulgaria, Latvia, and the Ukraine has the rate of natural population loss exceeded that of Russia.[3] The

[3] "Natural population loss" occurs when deaths exceed births. The rate of this loss is calculated by dividing the excess of deaths over births by the estimated midyear population. Other nations currently experiencing natural population loss are Belarus, Bulgaria, the Czech Republic, Estonia, Georgia, Germany, Hungary, Italy, Latvia, Lithuania, the Isle of Man, Monaco, Romania, Slovenia, Sweden, and the Ukraine (U.S. Census Bureau, 2000).

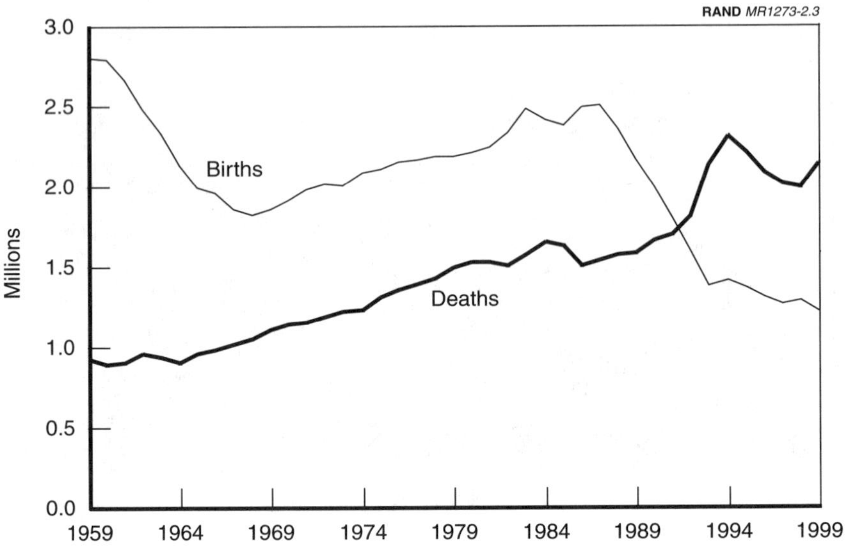

SOURCE: INED (2000).

Figure 2.3—Births and Deaths in Russia, 1959–99

rise in mortality rates in Russia is unprecedented for an industrialized nation at peace (Notzon et al., 1998).

Russian fertility traditionally has been higher in rural areas than elsewhere.[4] This has led to a larger rate of natural population increase in the sparsely populated areas of northern and eastern Russia than elsewhere (Figure 2.4). Of the 18 of 89 oblasts, or local administrative districts, that experienced a natural population increase in 1997, 12 had population densities of fewer than seven persons per square kilometer. Still, natural population increases here have not been enough to offset population losses from net out-migration.

---

4 In every year since at least 1959, the total fertility rate has been higher in rural than in urban areas (INED, 2000).

RAND MR1273-2.4

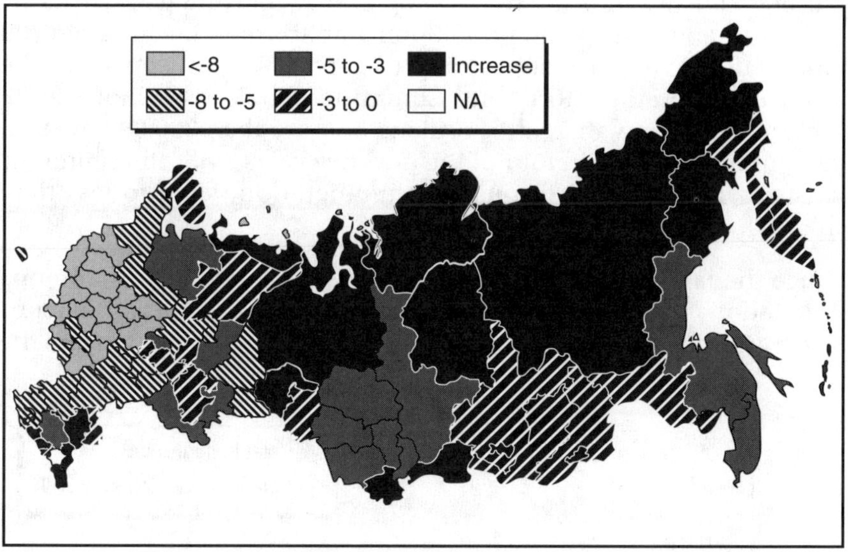

SOURCE: Pashintseva et al. (1998).

Figure 2.4—Natural Population Change Per 1,000 Population by Region, 1997

IMMIGRATION

Net immigration has not been able to offset natural population losses, but it has been able to keep the total population from dropping even more than it has. In 1994, for example, there were 2.3 million deaths and only 1.4 million births across Russia. In that year, net immigration[5] to Russia was its peak, with 1.15 million immigrants arriving in Russia and less than 340,000 emigrants departing. This meant that, rather than suffering a population loss of about 900,000 that year, Russia suffered a population loss of less than 100,000.

---

5 "Net immigration" is the population growth resulting from a higher level of immigration than emigration.

Recent statistics indicate that immigration is declining and, as a result, is unable to provide population stabilization, because natural population losses are continuing (Figure 2.5). Statistics from the Russian Federation (RF) State Committee on Statistics, or the RF Goskomstat, show that, after peaking at more than 800,000 in 1994, net immigration fell in four of the next five years, with the economic crisis of 1998 helping to push net immigration down to less than 165,000.

Since the late 1970s there has been considerable migration among the nations that comprised the USSR, with the number of persons immigrating to Russia from these states far outnumbering the

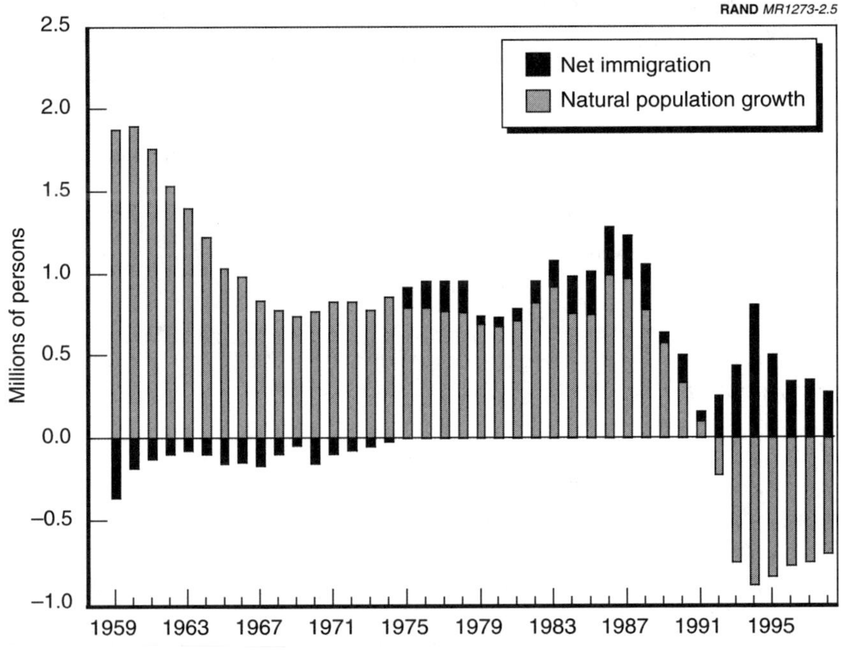

SOURCES: INED (2000); RF Goskomstat (1999b).

Figure 2.5—Natural Population Growth and Net Immigration in Russia, 1959–98

number emigrating from Russia to these states (Zaionchkovskaya, 1996).[6] This pattern continued after the fall of the Soviet Union. Between 1992 and 1998, total immigration from other states of the former Soviet Union to Russia was 5.545 million, while total emigration from Russia to other former states of the Soviet Union was 1.874 million, and total emigration from Russia to countries outside the former USSR was 698,000.[7] Most of the immigration to Russia has been by ethnic Russians (Figure 2.6).

Ethnic conflicts of the past decade have done much to determine the sources of immigration to the Soviet Union (Zayonchkovskaya, 1999a). Russians living outside Russia were most likely to migrate to Russia because of the ethnic discrimination they faced in the near abroad, including restrictions of their civil and political rights, curtailed use of the Russian language, and a shrinking number of managerial and professional positions available to ethnic Russians. Soviet policy of repatriating Russians from the near abroad had helped produce net immigration to Russia since the mid-1970s. Immigration sources, for Russians and others, have varied considerably, particularly as the locations of ethnic conflict change. Shortly before the fall of the USSR, ethnic conflicts in Azerbaijan, Uzbekistan, Tajikistan, and Kazakhstan spurred migration from these areas to Russia; these four former Soviet republics accounted for three-fourths of the net migration to Russia in 1990. After the demise of the Soviet Union, regions with armed conflicts—particularly the Transcaucasus, Moldova, and Tajikistan—saw large outflows of migrants to Russia. Since World War II, only the population movements on the Indian subcontinent following the departure of the British surpass in scale the internal population

---

[6] Again, all data that we cite, including those for the Soviet era, are for the territory that now comprises the Russian Federation. Much of the net immigration shown in Figure 2.5 was between Russia and other republics of the USSR.

[7] Most migration to Russia from 1992 to 1998 was from Kazakhstan (total immigration of 1.586 million) and the Ukraine (1.246 million). Most emigration from Russia to former Soviet states during this time was to the Ukraine (total emigration of 900,000). RF Goskomstat data show total immigration to Russia from countries that were outside the Soviet Union to total less than 3,000 between 1992 and 1998. Nearly all emigration between 1992 and 1998 from Russia to states outside the former Soviet Union was to Germany (total emigration of 451,000), Israel (120,000), and the United States (88,000). See RF Goskomstat (1999b).

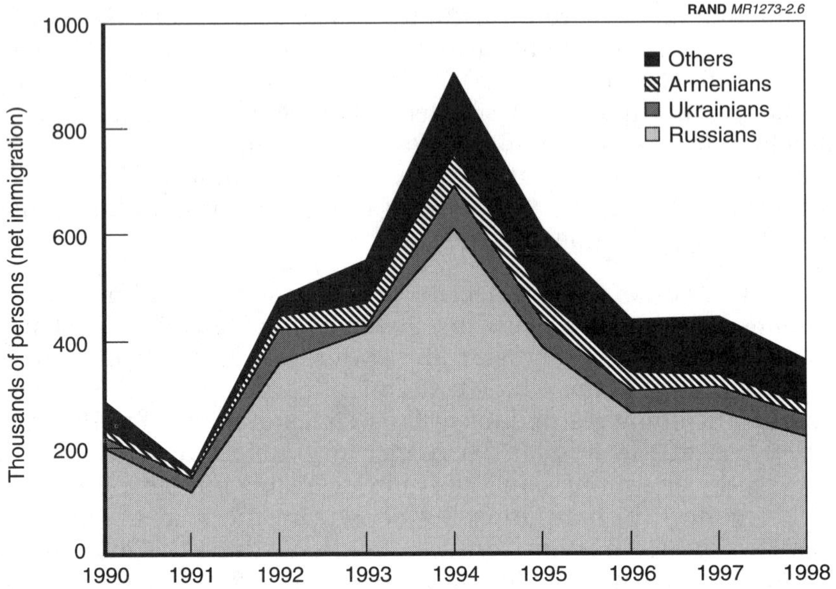

SOURCE: Fedorov (1999).

Figure 2.6—Net Immigration by Ethnicity between Russia and Other Former Soviet Republics[8]

movements that resulted from the demise of the Soviet Union (Burke, 2000).

Not surprisingly, much of the net immigration to Russia has occurred in borderlands, particularly near Kazakhstan and the Ukraine (Figure 2.7). More densely populated areas in the west also tend to have higher net immigration rates than other areas.

One problem that Russia and some potential recipient countries feared that does not appear to have materialized to the extent

[8] The net immigration shown in this graph is higher than that to which we earlier referred in the text because this graph shows the excess of immigrants over emigrants only for former Soviet republics, and not the immigration balance between Russia and all nations of the world.

RAND MR1273-2.7

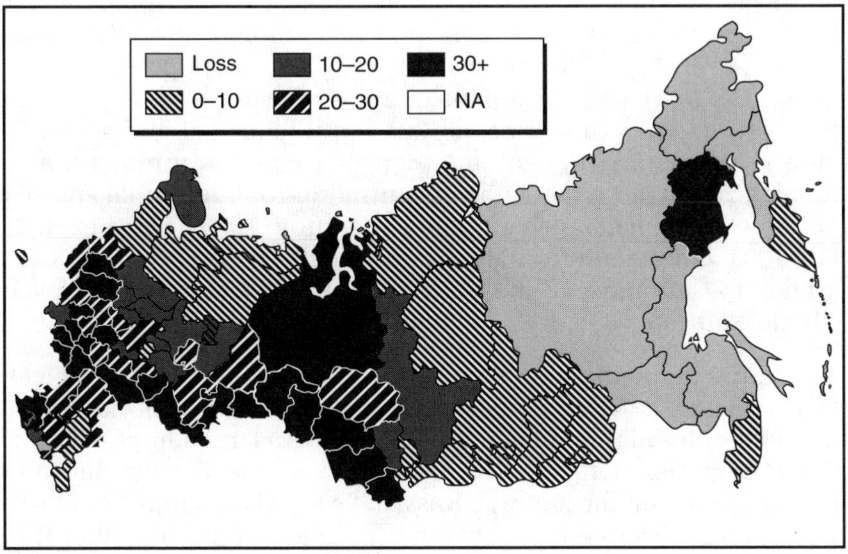

SOURCE: Pashintseva et al. (1998).

Figure 2.7—Net International Immigration per 10,000 Population by Region, 1997

previously feared is a massive "brain drain." Some analysts estimated that emigration from the former Soviet Union could total between 2.5 million and 7 million persons after the dissolution of the USSR, with a concentration among highly skilled workers such as scientists and mathematicians.[9] There has been little evidence to date,

[9] For analysis of "brain drain" fears in the early 1990s, see Shkolnikov (1995). Shkolnikov found that few emigrants of the early 1990s held postbaccalaureate degrees. In an analysis of emigration attitudes and intentions by aerospace engineers, nuclear engineers, and physicists, Shkolnikov predicted that emigration of these workers, while potentially damaging to the Russian economy, would be less than expected. He noted that those most likely to leave were the most entrepreneurial and those most supportive of social and economic reforms in Russia. In other words, the advancement of reforms or greater entrepreneurial opportunities in Russia would help cut potential emigration. He speculated that tight job markets in Western nations for some specializations (e.g., for defense workers) would also work to limit potential emigration, as would incompatibilities in Soviet and Western education. Yurevich and Tsapenko (1998) find that the character of recent "brain drain" has changed from that of earlier years, noting "the present intellectual emigration from Russia consists

however, of a substantial "brain drain." In fact, recent immigrants to Russia have a slightly higher average level of education than emigrants have (Zayonchkovskaya, 1999a). There is popular concern about the "brain drain" from major cities such as Moscow and Saint Petersburg, where much of the Russian intellectual and scientific elite is concentrated, but such concern ignores immigration to Russia from major cities with concentrations of intellectual and scientific elite in neighboring nations (Fedorov, 1999). Between 1992 and 1998, emigration from Russia declined by 68 percent, with emigration to Germany and the United States in 1998 below 1992 levels (RF Goskomstat, 1999b).[10]

The future demographic role of immigration in Russia is not clear. Historically, Russia has been a source of emigrants rather than a destination for immigrants. Russia may still have a large source of ethnic Russian immigrants in central Asia (Vitkovskaya, 1999). It may also be, however, that most ethnic Russians who wish to move to Russia from other Soviet lands have done so. The total immigration flow into the Russian Federation appears to be far less than the 25 million some projected in 1991, and future flows may have different ethnic mixes (Zayonchkovskaya, 1999b). There are now political pressures for the eventual "closure" or cessation of immigration, and RF Goskomstat population projections assume a drastic decline in net immigration by 2010 (Vishnevskii, 1999).

Russian desires for such "closure" point to the limits of immigration for population stability. Most Russians have been unaware of or indifferent to the role of immigration in stabilizing the size of the

---

mainly of junior researchers without degrees." Intellectual emigrants are now more likely to leave for Third World than Western nations, and for material reasons (e.g., greater salaries) than professional ones (e.g., lack of resources for research in Russia). A more significant problem for the current development of Russian science may be what Tsapenko and Yurevich (1999) call "internal brain drain," or the decision of Russian scientists to leave science for business within Russia, often in Western-owned firms.

[10] Emigration to Israel, the second most popular destination for Russian emigrants, has been more volatile. From nearly 22,000 persons in 1992, emigration to Israel fell to about 14,000 in 1995 and gradually increased to 17,000 by 1998 (RF Goskomstat, 1999b). Emigration to Israel reached nearly 30,000 in 1999, likely in response to increasing anti-Semitism and the 1998 economic crisis, but preliminary data show it dropping by half in 2000, perhaps in response to improving economic conditions and support by the Putin government of Jewish cultural activities (Lagnado, 1999; Goldberg, 2000b).

population (Fedorov, 1999).[11] Immigration of non-Russian populations often stirs popular opposition and concern. More than half (56 percent) of all Russians see at least some "threat to security of Russia from people of other nationalities living in Russia" (Russian Center for Public Opinion and Market Research, 2000). Russians are particularly concerned about threats posed by China and Chinese emigration to Russia. Nearly one in four (23 percent) Russians think China "could be a substantial threat to the security of Russia" (Russian Center for Public Opinion and Market Research, 2000). Chinese immigration to the Russian Far East has raised security concerns and resulted in a strong nationalist reaction, despite pressing labor needs in the region (Minakir, 1996; Zayonchkovskaya, 1999b; Working, 2000). Immigrants of non-Russian ethnicity, particularly those from the Caucausus, also have been viewed suspiciously in Moscow, with some Moscow journalists contributing to popular xenophobia and negative national stereotypes (Mereu, 2000; Badkhen, 2000).

If Russian immigration cannot be increased, the only other alternatives for population stability are to increase birth rates or to reduce death rates. The next two chapters discuss fertility and mortality rates in Russia.

---

[11] Some Russian demographers have advocated immigration to bolster the working-age population, but they have not been able to persuade the government of the need for such a policy. Vishnevskii (1999) writes, "Russia is precisely in need of population influx. This requirement is not being met even in general outline today. A clear-cut immigration policy has not been elaborated in this country, and to the extent that one is being pursued, it is restrictive in nature and aimed at limiting population influxes." The issue of replacement immigration has risen elsewhere in Europe as well. See, for example, McCarthy (2001).

Chapter Three

FERTILITY IN RUSSIA

TRENDS IN FERTILITY

Russian fertility rates have declined sharply since the breakup of the Soviet Union. The fall in Russian fertility, however, predates the past decade. Russian fertility rates have fallen throughout the 20th century. At the end of the 19th century, the total fertility rate in Russia, or the average number of children a woman would bear in her lifetime given age-specific fertility rates of the time, exceeded seven children per woman (Zakharov and Ivanova, 1996). By the end of the 20th century, the total fertility rate in Russia had fallen to about 1.2 children per woman (INED, 2000).

Declining fertility rates are not unique to Russia. Since the 1950s, fertility rates have fallen throughout Europe and North America and are now below replacement level[1] in a number of nations (Figure 3.1).

There are some unique characteristics of fertility trends in Russia. A postwar Soviet emphasis on economic development through heavy industrialization led to reduced birth rates by not only bringing more women into the workforce but also stifling the development of consumer goods industries that helped families in other nations to manage the demands of work and home (Stloukal, 1999).

---

1 "Replacement level" fertility is reached when, on average, women give birth to 2.1 children in their lifetime.

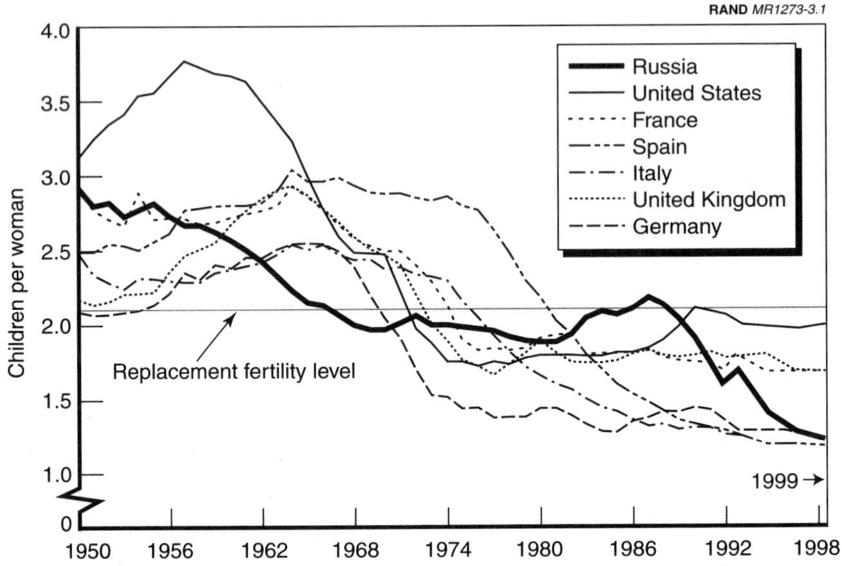

SOURCES: Vishnevsky (1996) for pre-1993 data; U.S. Census Bureau (2000) for post-1992 data.

Figure 3.1—Total Fertility Rate in Russia and Six Western Nations

Prior to 1980, the Russian fertility rate was declining slowly while the total number of Russian births was climbing. This was due to a growing number of women of reproductive age who had been born in the previous generation. These women were each typically having fewer children than the generation of women before them, but, because there were more of them, the number of newborns grew. This "population momentum" has been exhausted, and the long-term decline in Russian fertility rates is now yielding a rapidly declining total number of births and large natural population losses.

The last period of increase for the Russian fertility rate was from 1980 to 1987, when the total fertility rate increased by 0.36 children per woman, briefly surpassing the level of replacement fertility. During this period, the Soviet government instituted several pronatalist policies. Paid maternity leave was extended from one to three years. The definition of "large families" eligible for housing and medical benefits was changed from families of five children to those with three. This made it more beneficial for families with two children to have a third child than it had been previously.

The coincidence of pronatalist incentives and higher fertility rates in the 1980s has led some (e.g., Perevedentsev, 1999; United Nations Economic Commission for Europe, 2000) to suggest expanded pronatalist policies as a way for Russia to increase its birth rate.[2] Russian politicians are also seeking to reintroduce Soviet-era incentives for large families and "hero mothers" of many children (Harrigan, 2000). Indeed, the Soviet Union had a history of explicitly pronatalist incentives dating to 1936 (Popov and David, 1999).

There is no evidence, however, of success for pronatalist policies, either in Russia or elsewhere. No nation instituting pronatalist policies in response to below-replacement fertility levels has yet been able to sustain such policies to the point that they raised fertility to replacement levels or above for more than a few years. Although Russian fertility rates initially increased following the introduction of pronatalist incentives in the 1930s and 1940s, they then declined throughout the 1950s, 1960s, and 1970s (Popov and David, 1999).

The decline in Russian fertility in the past decade probably is attributable in part to timing effects of the pronatalist incentives of the 1980s. That is, it is likely that the pronatalist incentives induced many couples to have children earlier than they would have otherwise, helping to accelerate the subsequent decline in fertility rates after these couples had achieved their desired family size (Zakharov and Ivanova, 1996). Rather than reflecting fundamental changes in fertility behavior, the increase in fertility resulting from Soviet pronatalist policies appears to have been mainly a result of women spacing their births closer together rather than increasing the number of children that they would ultimately have. The higher age-specific fertility rates of the 1980s, which are used to calculate the total fertility rate, thus caused a distorted view of overall Russian fertility trends.

---

[2] The Russian government has pledged $125 million in pronatalist incentives in the next two years (Heleniak, 2001a).

To be sure, the economic conditions of the 1990s appear to have had their own effect on Russian fertility rates. Whereas the Russian total fertility rate in the early 1990s was comparable to that of France and the United Kingdom, and just below that of the United States, today it is among the lowest in the world. Poor economic conditions in the 1990s probably have contributed to lower fertility rates in Russia by making couples less able to afford to raise children and generally less optimistic about bringing them into the world. Many of the costs of raising children (child care, food, education, and housing) have increased substantially since the breakup of the Soviet Union (Heleniak, 2001a). Nearly half (46 percent) of all Russians rate their "family's present material condition" as "bad" or "very bad" (Russian Center for Public Opinion and Market Research, 2000). Less than half (48 percent) say their family has "adapted to the changes that happened in the country during the last ten years," and most (53 percent) do not expect improvement for their family in the near future.

Birth rates do not decline solely because of economic troubles, however. Among the few nations with fertility rates as low as that for Russia, for example, are Spain and Italy. Both these nations have seen great economic improvements in recent decades but now have fertility rates of less than 1.2 children per woman. Within Eastern Europe, economic recovery in the 1990s in nations such as Hungary and Poland has not reversed fertility rate declines (Figure 3.2).

Within Russia, fertility rates vary considerably by region, with areas in the east and the south, particularly Siberia and the Caucasus, having higher birth rates than other areas, and those near Saint Petersburg and Moscow having among the lowest (Figure 3.3). There are also some ethnic dimensions to Russian fertility rates. Those areas with the highest concentrations of Islamic religious communities have crude birth rates (rates of birth per 1,000 population) about a fourth higher than those for other areas of Russia (Krindatch, 1996; Pashintseva, Voronina, and Kazachenko, 1998). More generally, rural Russian women have higher fertility levels than urban Russian women have, although even the average fertility level for rural women has been below replacement level since 1993 (INED, 2000). Regional variation in birth rates correlates highly with that in natural population increase discussed earlier, but it is negatively related to

RAND MR1273-3.2

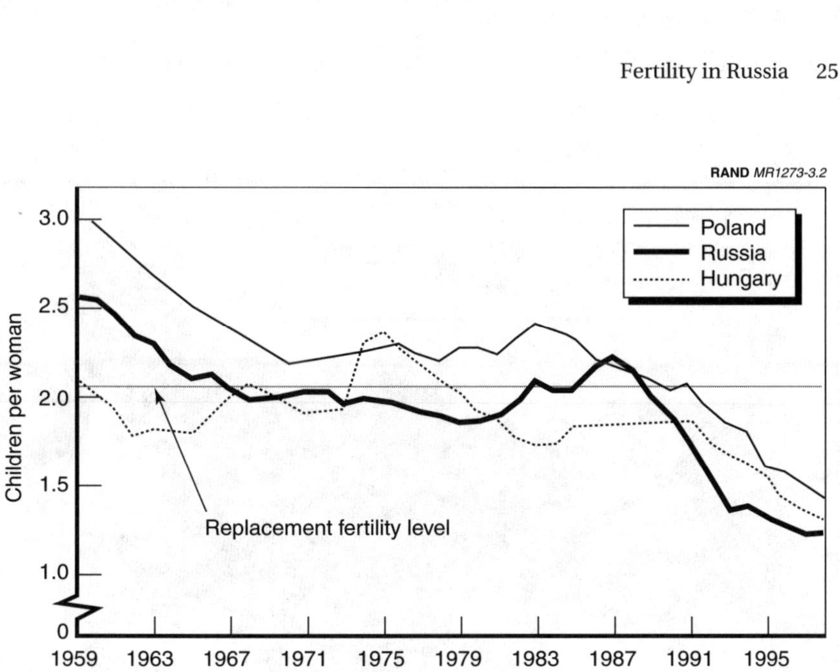

SOURCE: DaVanzo and Grammich (2000).

Figure 3.2—Total Fertility Rate in Russia, Hungary, and Poland

total population growth. That is, the regions with the highest birth rates have not had enough births to offset population losses resulting from net out-migration.

ABORTION AND CONTRACEPTION

In addition to having one of the lowest fertility rates in the world, Russia has one of the highest abortion rates (David, 1999). In the mid-1990s, nearly 7 in 100 Russian women of childbearing age had an abortion each year, a rate about three times that for U.S. women (Figure 3.4). For several reasons, including an inability to develop an open market for effective contraceptive services, many current and formerly communist countries have among the highest rates of abortion in the world. Vietnam, Romania, and Cuba are estimated to have even higher rates of abortion than that of Russia, and China is estimated to have a higher total number of abortions (Wulf, 1999). Some Russian women have had 10 or more abortions in their lifetime;

RANDMR1273-3.3.eps

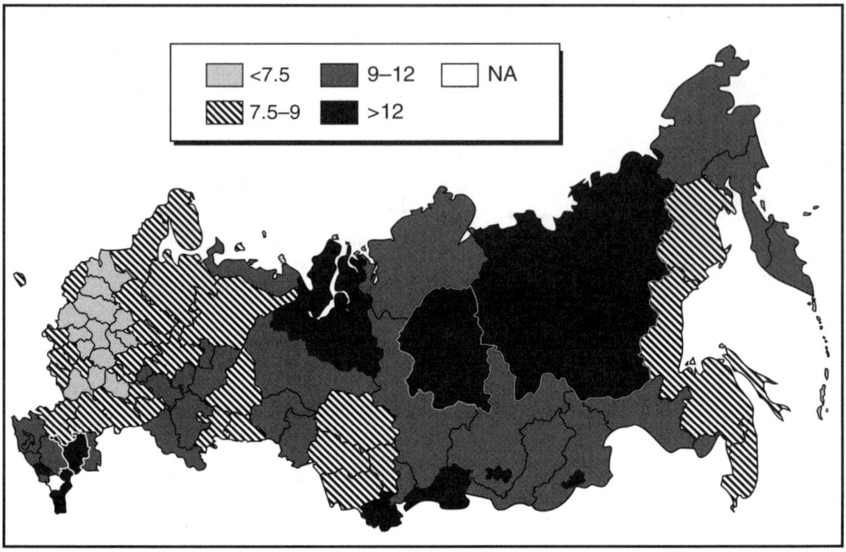

SOURCE: Pashintseva et al. (1998).

Figure 3.3—Crude Birth Rate[3] (Births per 1,000 Population) by Region, 1997

more than three in four Russian women who have ever been pregnant have had an abortion (Popov and David, 1999). A 1994 survey found that Russian women at the end of their childbearing years (i.e., those 45 to 49 years old) had obtained an average of 3.2 abortions in their lifetime (Entwistle and Kozyreva, 1997). In 1997, about seven in ten Russian pregnancies ended in abortion (Agence France Presse,

[3] We map the crude birth rate, or the number of births per 1,000 population, because this statistic is more widely available on a regional level than is the total fertility rate. Published data (Pashintseva, Voronina, and Kazachenko, 1998) allow calculation of crude birth rates for every region but Chechnya, but provide total fertility rates for only 79 of the 89 oblast-level areas in the Russian Federation. There is, of course, a very high level of correlation between crude birth rates and total fertility rates (r=0.98 in the RF Goskomstat data). Because crude birth rates are also affected by the age and sex composition of the population, total fertility rates are usually more suitable for analysis of fertility behavior.

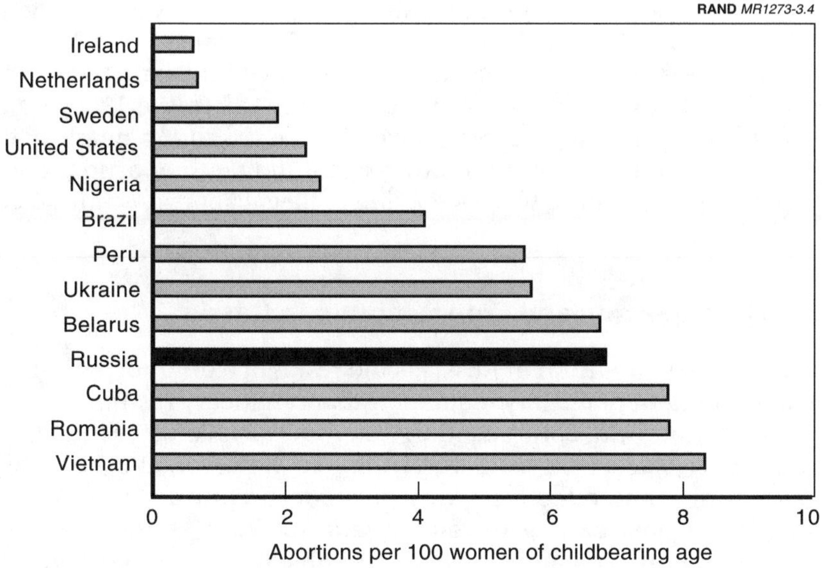

SOURCE: Wulf (1999).

Figure 3.4—Abortion Rates in Selected Countries, 1995–96

1998). By contrast, less than three in ten U.S. pregnancies end in abortion (U.S. Census Bureau, 1999).

High rates of abortion in Russia have led to myriad health problems. Overall, two in three Russian women aborting their pregnancies suffer health complications as a result of the procedure, placing strain on the Russian health system (Agence France Presse, 1998). Abortion has led to high rates of secondary sterility in Russia. There are estimates that one in ten Russian women are left sterile by the procedure; in Khabarovsk Kray in the Far East, some estimate that one in five minors undergoing the procedure, for example, suffer secondary sterility as a result (Bazhenova, 2001a; Klyshnikov, 1999). Abortion is a principal cause of maternal mortality in Russia, accounting for more than one in four maternal deaths in the early 1990s (Kingkade, 1997; Meslé et al., 1996; Popov and David, 1999). About 90 percent of maternal deaths in Russia attributable to abortion are the result of illegal abortions, i.e., abortions performed by somebody without the appropriate license. Even though abortion is legal in Russia, illegal abortions sometimes are sought for confidentiality. Deaths attributable to abortion have declined, as the procedure, particularly in clandestine settings, has become less frequent.[4] In the 1960s and 1970s, when abortion was more prevalent than it is today, nearly half of all maternal deaths in Russia were attributable to abortion, and more than 95 percent of these were due to illegal abortions (Meslé et al., 1996).

History of Abortion and Contraception in Russia

The high rate of abortion in Russia is the result of a unique pattern in the development of fertility regulation there (Avdeev, 1994). In most nations of the world, contraception was widely available or used before abortion was legally available. In Russia, however, abortion was legal before many effective forms of modern contraception were widely available, leading to reliance on abortion as the primary means of fertility regulation, despite the substantial health problems for women caused by high abortion rates.

The Soviet Union first legalized abortion in 1920. Widespread famine at that time led many couples, desiring to limit their fertility but lacking effective means of contraception, to resort to abortion. The goal of abortion legalization was to limit the number of abortions performed outside hospitals so as to reduce maternal morbidity and mortality; prior to legalization, about one in five Russian pregnancies was aborted (Popov and David, 1999). This policy was successful in reducing maternal mortality and morbidity, but the availability of abortion, which physicians provided freely at state hospitals, coupled with the lack of widespread contraception, made abortion the most frequently used means of fertility regulation.

Soviet ideology inadvertently reinforced this preference. It held that declining fertility rates were not typical of socialism and that socialist economic improvement would yield higher birth rates and lower abortion rates. Such views resulted in little attention or effort being

---

[4] Although there are no complete data on the number of illegal abortions between 1991 and 1996 (the most recent year for which any such data are available), it appears that the number of illegal abortions declined at about twice the rate as that for other abortions (Avdeev and Troitskaia, 1999).

made to the development or dissemination of modern contraceptive methods in Russia.

Contrary to Soviet expectations, the number of abortions continued to rise, and the number of births continued to fall, into the 1930s. By the mid-1930s in Moscow there were nearly three abortions for every birth (Lorimer, 1946). Because of these trends, and because of population losses resulting from forced collectivization and starvation, the Stalin government, in 1936, sought to encourage more births by prohibiting abortion. In 1955, two years after the death of Stalin, the Supreme Soviet repealed his prohibitions against the procedure, citing in part the need to reduce "the harm caused to the health of women by abortions performed outside of hospitals" (Popov and David, 1999). Still, Soviet authorities continued to view abortion and low fertility rates as temporary phenomena in a socialist society.

Russian abortion rates climbed rapidly after relegalization, in part because of increasing urbanization and the desires of urban couples for smaller families. By 1965, the total number of abortions had climbed to 5.5 million, and the abortion rate had risen to more than 16 abortions per 100 women of childbearing age (Popov, 1996).[5] That is, about one in six women of childbearing age had an abortion that year. By contrast, fewer than 1 in 30 women of childbearing age in the United States have had an abortion in any single year since the *Roe v. Wade* decision legalizing abortion (U.S. Census Bureau, 1999).

With three in four pregnancies ending in abortion in the mid-1960s, Soviet health planners finally recognized low fertility and small family sizes as a reaction to economic development and declining mortality levels and that, contrary to ideological expectations, socialism would not inevitably lead to higher fertility rates. Russian couples, like couples around the world, had seen that declining rates of infant

[5] Although the Soviet Union gathered and published extensive statistics on abortion after legalizing the procedure, for most of its history it suppressed data on abortion, declining to publish official data from 1929 to 1988. Changes in registration systems can also distort abortion statistics. Readers wishing to know more about Soviet and Russian statistics, their compilation and publication, and possible distortions in them should consult Popov and David (1999), especially pp. 242–246, and Popov (1996). INED (2000) data publications that we use to analyze trends in Russian abortion rates also provide discussion of Russian abortion statistics, their variations, and possible biases.

mortality and increasing life expectancy meant they could have fewer births to achieve their desired number of surviving offspring. Soviet health planners sought to induce Russian couples to use contraception rather than abortion to do so. Intrauterine devices (IUDs), for example, whose use Soviet medical handbooks of the 1950s had discouraged, began to be available in limited qualities in the late 1960s (Popov and David, 1999).

While making more contraceptives available, however, Soviet planners paid little attention to contraceptive quality or distribution (Popov and David, 1999). Oral contraceptives were available only in high-dosage pills imported from Central and Eastern Europe, and their use led to many side effects. Diaphragms were manufactured in only one size, and Russian-produced condoms made of thick dark latex were unpleasant to use. Erratic supply problems were particularly pronounced in rural areas. There were contraceptive market difficulties in Russia during the early 1990s, when the only two condom factories stopped production because they could not afford to import latex, and the single factory producing IUDs shut over concern about the quality of its products. The poor quality of Russian-made contraceptives, as well as popular fears of deleterious health effects resulting from use of hormonal contraceptives, reinforced preferences for abortion over contraception into the 1990s (Brown, 1997; Bohlen, 1999).

Soviet medical practitioners also faced incentives that kept abortion rates high. Until the late 1980s, obtaining a legal abortion required a subsequent three-day hospital stay (Peterson, 1987). Because Soviet hospitals were financed in part according to their number of occupied beds, and because Soviet medical care focused on curative rather than preventive treatments, medical practitioners were more likely to perform abortion than to encourage contraception (Rozenfeld, 1996; Goldberg et al., 1998; Twigg, 2000). The requirement of a hospital stay had another consequence: It led to a large number of illegal abortions for women seeking greater confidentiality. Hospital stays were no longer legally required once "mini-abortions," or abortion by "regulation of a menstrual cycle by vacuum-aspiration," were legalized in 1988 (Popov, 1996). Nonetheless, the profits to be made from performing abortion continue to be a strong disincentive for low-paid physicians in post-Soviet Russia to encourage contraception (Popov and David, 1999).

Recent Declines in Abortion

Despite the formal and informal cultural and economic incentives to abortion, both the abortion rate, or the number of abortions per 100 women of childbearing age, and the abortion ratio, or the number of abortions per 100 live births, have declined in recent decades (Figure 3.5). The decline in the abortion rate has helped Russia cut health problems that might arise from the procedure, while the decline (excepting the late 1980s and early 1990s) in the abortion ratio suggests that fewer Russian pregnancies are unintended.

RAND *MR1273-3.5*

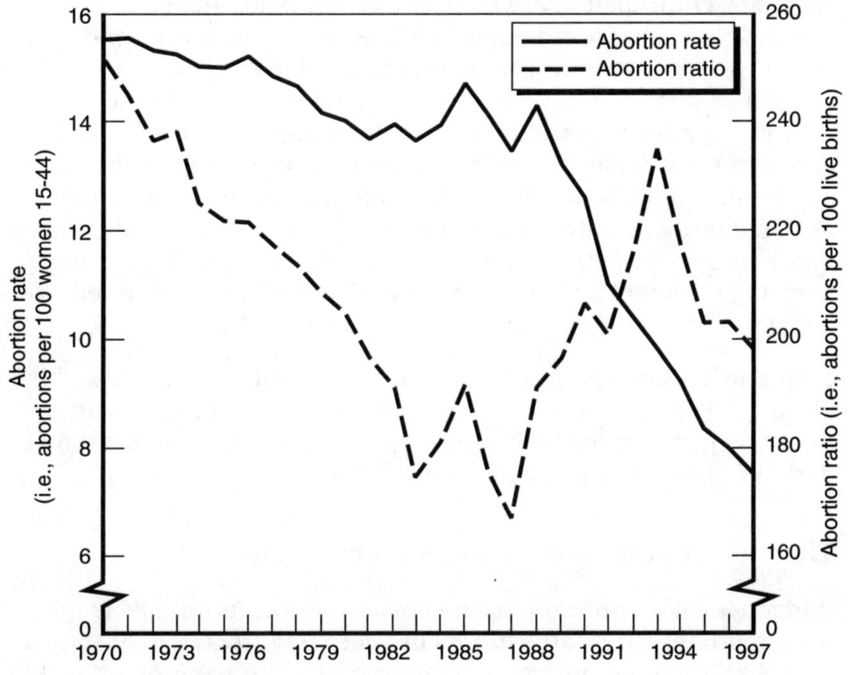

SOURCE: INED (2000).

Figure 3.5—Russian Abortion Rates and Ratios, 1970–97

The abortion rate has dropped sharply since 1988. The abortion ratio increased from 1987 to 1993, and has declined since then. Pronatalist incentives may have contributed to this seeming anomaly. The abortion rate, based on the number of women of childbearing age, tends not to change much year to year, while the abortion ratio, based on the number of births in a given year, can change greatly in a short time. The number of abortions decreased immediately after pronatalist incentives were instituted, while the number of births increased. This caused both the abortion rate and the abortion ratio to decline. Pregnancies that otherwise might have been aborted may have been brought to term because of the incentives. The number of abortions continued to decrease in the late 1980s and early 1990s, so the abortion rate continued to decline. The events surrounding the fall of the Soviet Union, however, saw the number of births drop more sharply than the number of abortions, leading to increases in the ratio of abortions to live births. This suggests that the number of desired births declined, but the number of pregnancies did not fall correspondingly. Since 1994, the annual number of abortions has declined more rapidly than the number of births has declined, causing the abortion ratio to decline again. This suggests that women have been increasingly successful in preventing unintended pregnancies.

Today in Russia there are two induced abortions per live birth. Although this is far above the ratio of one abortion for about every three live births in the United States, it is considerably lower than the mid-1960s ratio of three abortions per live birth.

The Role of Contraception in Reducing Abortion

Wider availability of modern means of contraception has led to the decline in abortion rates in recent years (Figure 3.6). Not until the late 1980s did the number of women using contraception exceed the number who used abortion to prevent births.

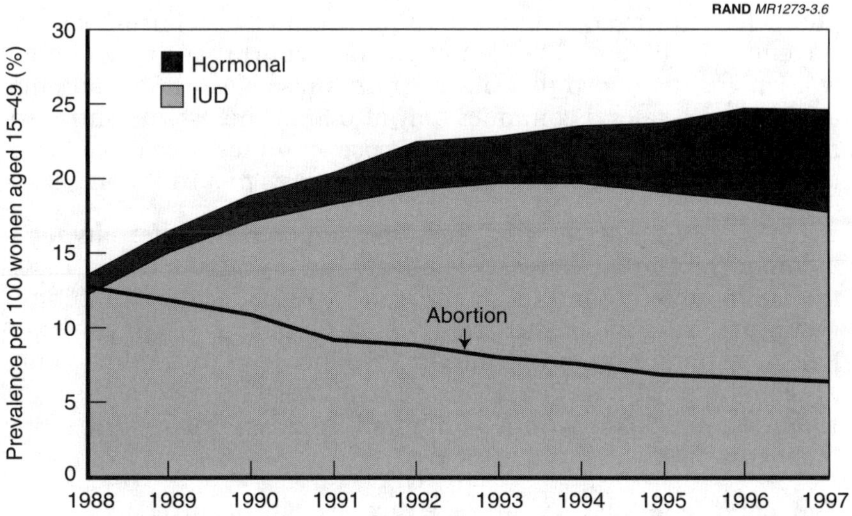

SOURCES: Avdeev and Troitskaia (1999); INED (2000); Zakharov (2000a).

Figure 3.6—Abortion and Contraceptive Use in Russia, 1988–97

Contraceptive use by Russian women has roughly doubled since 1988 (Avdeev and Troitskaia, 1999).[6] IUDs remain the most popular method of fertility regulation, with about eight million women using this method, but use of hormonal contraceptives (e.g., birth control pills) is growing rapidly, with about two million women using this method.

---

[6] Long-term data on IUD use show a very rapid rise in IUD use in the 1980s followed by a decline in the 1990s (Zakharov, 2000b). Between 1982 and 1989, the number of IUD users more than tripled, from about 588,000 to nearly 1.95 million, while the number of women of childbearing age declined by 0.9 percent. Between 1989 and 1999, the number of IUD users declined by nearly two-thirds, to just over 750,000, while the number of women of childbearing age increased 7.3 percent. Data on abortion are not available past 1997. Citing data from the Russian Federation Ministry of Health (1999), Zakharov (2000b) notes IUD use declined between 1997 and 1998 from 17.8 to 17.3 percent of women of childbearing age, while hormonal contraceptive use increased from 6.8 percent to 7.2 percent. Pre-1988 data on hormonal contraceptive usage are not available.

There may, however, be limits to the growth in use of hormonal contraceptives (Bohlen, 1999). Some doctors report that many Russian women are convinced that birth control pills cause cancer and that abortions are safer. Economics may also limit the use of contraception. After several years of increasing use, contraceptive use was unchanged in 1998, when a severe economic crisis rocked Russia.

Use of contraceptive sterilization, the main method of fertility regulation in the United States, is relatively rare in Russia. In the 1930s, the Stalin government, in an effort to increase fertility, prohibited voluntary surgical contraceptive sterilization (Popov, 1996). Relegalization of the procedure in 1990 included restrictions on its availability until 1993 (Popov and David, 1999). Between 1991 and 1998, about 90,000 women obtained contraceptive sterilization (Zakharov, 2000a).[7]

The increase in Russian contraceptive use has occurred as Russian fertility behavior has undergone a fundamental shift, becoming more like that in the West, with later marriages and still later bearing of children. Specifically, it was more common in the past than now for first sexual contact, first marriage, and first desired pregnancy to coincide for Russian couples (Zakharov, 1999c).[8] Such patterns of fertility behavior led many Russian couples to quickly reach their desired number of offspring and to abort all subsequent pregnancies. As these events have become more independent, Russian marriage rates have declined, and the proportion of Russian children born out of wedlock has risen (Popov and David, 1999). With first sexual contact, first marriage, and first childbirth becoming as independent in Russia as they are in the West, more Russian couples need contraceptive services.

---

[7] Data for Russian men undergoing voluntary surgical sterilization are not available. It is likely that this procedure is less common among males than females in Russia. In the United States, for example, female sterilization is used more than twice as often as a method of fertility regulation than is male sterilization (National Center for Health Statistics, 1999).

[8] While Russian birth rates are currently highest for 20–24-year-old women, Zakharov (1999b) projects that by 2015 they will be highest for 25–29-year-old women. This would fulfill in part what he considers the "second demographic transition" that has already occurred in western Europe, where mean age at first birth is in the late 20s, while that in Russia (and the United States) is in the early 20s.

Russian contraceptive access has increased in part through efforts by the Russian government and the United States Agency for International Development (USAID). A USAID program at selected sites since 1996 to expand the use of effective contraception and to reduce abortion and maternal mortality has led to declining abortion rates and increased contraceptive use among younger women (United States Agency for International Development, 2000). Russians also made significant strides in increasing contraception and reducing abortion through their Federal Family Planning Program, which increased the number of family planning clinics threefold between 1991 and 1997 (Fedorov, 1999). These efforts have helped Russia nearly achieve a freely operating market for contraceptives. Beyond helping to cut the abortion rate, increasing access to contraception and the resulting decline in the total number of pregnancies have helped improve maternal health care. With fewer pregnancies than in previous years, Russian women and infants are receiving much more attention to their health. Maternal mortality has declined by nearly a third in the 1990s, with that caused by abortion declining by more than half, and infant mortality has also decreased slightly (Bohlen, 1999; Pashintseva, Voronina, and Kazachenko, 1998).[9]

Reaction Against Contraception and Abortion

There is growing resistance to both abortion and family planning programs in Russia. Both to curb health problems resulting from abortion and to boost population growth, some Russian officials are seeking curbs on the procedure. The deputy premier for social affairs has called for a 10 percent reduction in the Russian abortion rate in order to boost population (Agence France Presse, 1998).[10]

---

[9] Nevertheless, there are indications that health problems of surviving newborns remain significant, particularly because of mothers' drinking and drug use, complications caused by sexually transmitted diseases, inadequate prenatal care, and a lack of medical equipment (Dolgov, 2000).

[10] At the same time, she recognized that economic conditions are making population growth difficult. A family with three young children, in which both parents work and earn an average wage, for example, struggles near poverty (Agence France Presse, 1998). Poverty for young children, i.e., those 0 to 6 years of age, climbed rapidly for much of the 1990s, with 56 percent living in poverty in November 1998, compared to 39 percent for all Russians (Mroz, Mancini, and Popkin, 1999).

Some militant Russian nationalists, seeing in declining birth rates and increasing death rates "a plot to smother Russia in its cradle," have, with the backing of the Russian Orthodox Church, campaigned successfully for reductions in funds for family planning programs (Bohlen, 1999). The Federal Family Planning Program received 92 percent of its appropriated funds between 1994 and 1996 but less than ten percent of its appropriations for 1997 (Fedorov, 1999). The chief obstetrician of the Russian Ministry of Health succinctly summarized the Russian political problems confronting family planning programs when he quoted lawmakers telling him "few enough of us were being born as it is, and then you come along with your [family planning] program" (Fedorov, 1999). Complicating these matters is strong resistance, dating from Communist days, to formal education on sexuality (Popov and David, 1999). Soviet schools offered no education on sexuality except for a brief, unsuccessful program in the 1980s. Education on sexuality issues was also absent from Soviet medical schools. Even today, few Russian schools are willing to go against public opinion opposing sexuality education.

Prospects for Future Fertility and Population Growth

Should fertility rates not fall substantially further, the number of Russian births may increase in the near future as the large cohorts born in the 1980s enter their childbearing years. The subsequent entry into these same ages of the smaller cohorts born in the 1990s, however, will likely create a negative population momentum shortly thereafter. The number of Russian women in their prime childbearing years, i.e., those in their 20s, is projected to grow 12 percent by 2009, but then to decline by nearly 40 percent between 2009 and 2020 (U.S. Census Bureau, 2000).

For now, there are other pressing population problems in Russia, particularly those indicated by high mortality levels, that may be more amenable to immediate policy initiatives. In the next chapter, we review these problems and what might be done about them.

Chapter Four

CAUSES AND IMPLICATIONS OF RUSSIAN MORTALITY

RUSSIAN POPULATION LOSSES AND DECLINING LIFE EXPECTANCY

Natural population growth occurs when births exceed deaths. For most of the 20th century, births in Russia have exceeded deaths, and the population has grown. The number of Russian births reached nearly 2.5 million in 1987, a year in which there were 1.5 million deaths, resulting in a natural population increase of about 1 million persons. Since then, the number of births has dropped sharply, due both to declining fertility rates and to declining numbers of women of childbearing age. The number of births in 1999, 1.2 million, was nearly 1 million less than the number of deaths in 1999 and half the 1987 level.

While the declining number of births is most responsible for recent population losses, the increasing number of deaths also has contributed to population losses. Between 1987 and 1994, the annual number of deaths in Russia increased from 1.5 million to 2.3 million. In seven of the past eight years there have been at least two million deaths in Russia. By contrast, for most of the 1960s the annual number of deaths in Russia was below one million, and in the 1970s the annual number of deaths never exceeded two million.

Population aging has contributed to increases in mortality; that is, a larger proportion of the Russian population is now of ages where mortality is higher. Yet age-specific mortality rates, or the mortality rates of each age group, have also increased, especially for working-age males. That is, working-age males now suffer higher rates of mortality than they did in past years. Higher age-specific mortality rates have led to declining life expectancy.

Statistics on life expectancy at birth help summarize health and mortality conditions for a population. Life expectancy at birth in a given year is a statistical calculation based on the age-specific mortality rates of that year. It reflects the number of years a child born in a particular year could be expected to live if the age-specific mortality rates of that year apply throughout the child's life. By calculating life expectancies for different population groups (e.g., males and females, Russians and others), we can summarize health and mortality conditions for these groups. Life expectancies are better than crude death rates, or the raw number of deaths per 1,000 population in a given year, for comparing mortality conditions across time or place, because crude death rates can be affected by differences in population age structure, with older populations having higher crude death rates.

Life expectancies for males and females in Russia, and Russian health conditions generally, improved from the 1920s through the early 1960s (Figure 4.1). During this time, the life expectancy for both Russian males and females increased by nearly 30 years. Whereas before World War II Russian life expectancy had trailed that for the United States by nearly 20 years, by the mid-1960s it was nearly equal to that of the United States for both men and women. Since then, however, Russian life expectancy has been static or has declined, while that in the United States has continued to improve. Russian female life expectancy today is eight years lower than that for U.S. women. Russian male life expectancy is 14 years lower than that for U.S. men, and is also lower than that for males in Guatemala, Indonesia, Iraq, Mexico, Morocco, and the Philippines (U.S. Census Bureau, 2000). We will explore the reasons for recent variations in Russian life expectancy, particularly for working-age males, during the period of improvement from 1984 to 1987, decline from 1987 to 1992, sharp decline from 1992 to 1994, and improvement from 1994 to 1996.

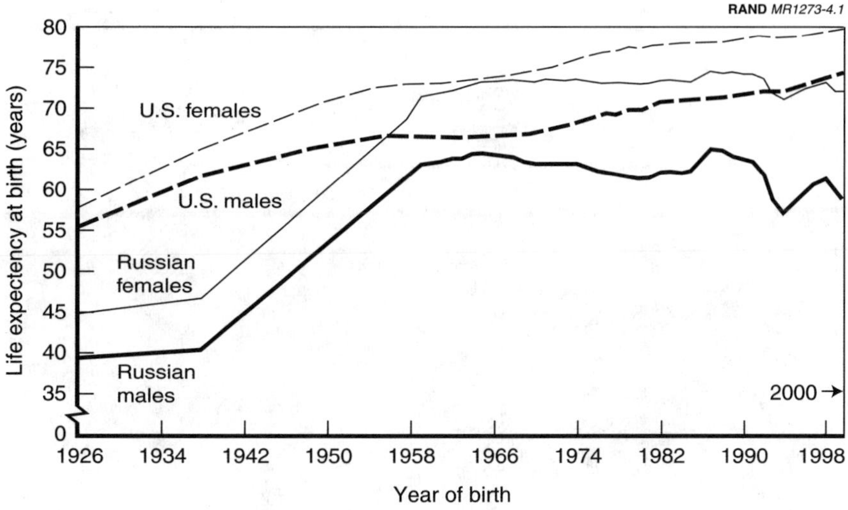

SOURCES: Shkolnikov and Meslé (1996); U.S. Census Bureau (2000); Gorbacheva (2001).

Figure 4.1—Trends in Russian and U.S. Life Expectancy by Sex, 1926–2000

There is considerable variation in life expectancy by region within Russia, with life expectancies for both sexes combined in 1997 ranging from 56 to 73 years (Figure 4.2). Life expectancies are generally lower in Siberia, the Far East, and the North regions, and higher in the southwest, particularly in the Caucasus, Volga, and Black Soil regions. As we will see, there are different reasons for this variation in life expectancy, which indicate different problems the Russian health care system faces in each area. Sparsely populated Siberia and the Far East, for example, have higher levels of infant mortality, indicating problems with basic provision of medical services, while several oblasts in the North and Northwest regions have high levels of working-age mortality, indicating greater problems in combating "civilization" ills such as cardiovascular diseases.

RAND *MR1273-4.2*

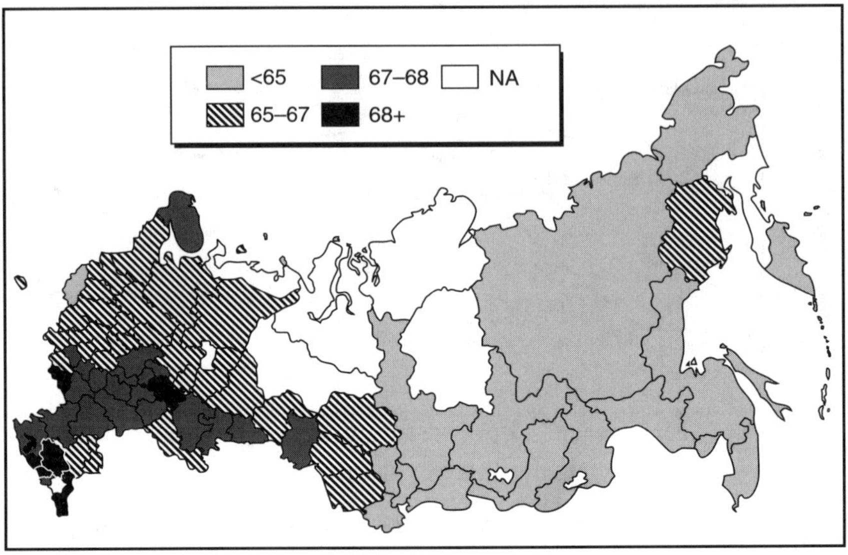

SOURCE: Pashintseva et al. (1998).

Figure 4.2—Russian Life Expectancy by Region, 1997

INCREASING MORTALITY FOR WORKING-AGE MALES

Recent Russian health problems, particularly those resulting from "civilization" diseases, have not stricken all equally. Life expectancy has declined more for males than females, particularly in recent years. Provisional data indicate that Russian males born in 2000 had a life expectancy of 58.9 years, while that for Russian women was 72.0 years (Gorbacheva, 2001). This difference in life expectancy by sex is among the largest in the world. In only seven other nations do differences in life expectancy by sex exceed ten years; six of these were formerly in the Soviet Union (U.S. Census Bureau, 2000).[1]

---

[1] Former Soviet states where female life expectancy exceeds that for males by at least ten years are Belarus, Estonia, Kazakhstan, Latvia, Lithuania, and Ukraine. The only other nation where female life expectancy is at least ten years greater than that for males is Seychelles.

At the root of the decline in Russian life expectancy is an increase in mortality for working-age persons, particularly working-age males. Changes in life expectancy from mortality in each age and sex group have been greatest among persons 35 to 64, particularly among males in those age groups (Figure 4.3). Between 1990 and 1994, mortality increases among males aged 35–44, 45–54, and 55–64 were so great as to reduce overall male life expectancy by more than a year each. In 1994, a 20-year-old Russian male had a 1 in 2 chance of surviving to age 60, compared with a 9 in 10 chance for a 20-year-old male in the United States or Great Britain (Leon and Shkolnikov, 1998).

Although rising most rapidly in the early 1990s, Russian working-age male mortality has been increasing steadily since the mid-1960s, well before the breakup of the Soviet Union (Figure 4.4). Despite wide

RAND *MR1273-4.3*

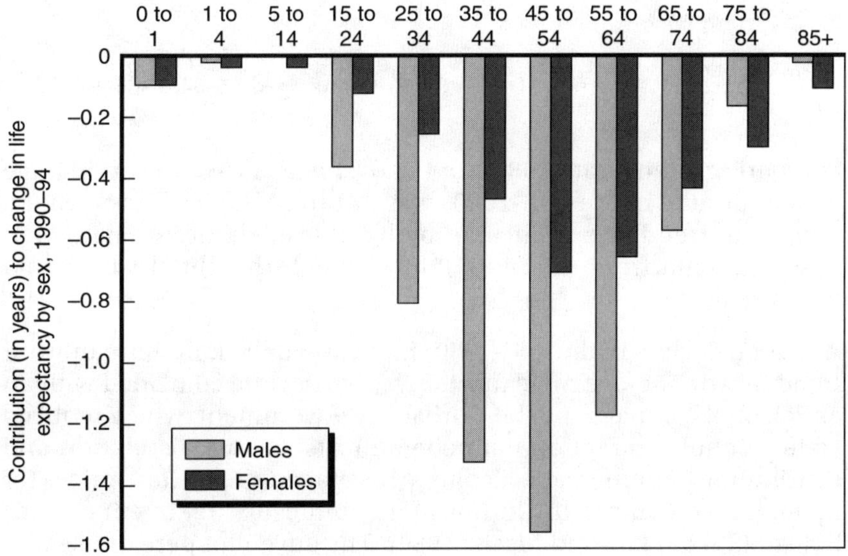

SOURCE: Nortzon et al. (1998).

Figure 4.3—Mortality Increases by Age and Sex and Their Contribution to Changes in Life Expectancy by Sex, 1990–94

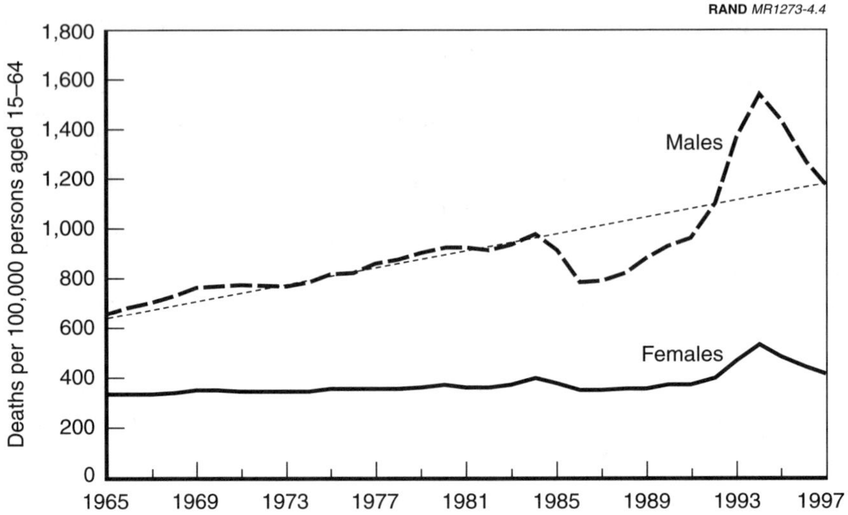

SOURCES: Meslé at al. (1996); Pashintseva et al. (1998); U.S. Census Bureau (2000).

Figure 4.4—Mortality by Sex for Russians Aged 15–64, 1965–97

fluctuations in the late 1980s and early 1990s, Russian working-age male mortality in the mid-1990s was not that different from what a long-term trend line (indicated by light dashed line in Figure 4.4) based on data from the mid-1960s through the mid-1980s would have predicted.

A sudden decline in the mid-1980s interrupted the long-term upward trend in working-age male mortality. This decline coincided with an antialcohol campaign by the Gorbachev government, which reduced state alcohol production, launched efforts against distillation and distribution of homemade alcoholic beverages, raised state prices for liquor, and enhanced institutions for compulsory treatment of alcoholism (Shkolnikov and Meslé, 1996). The advent of perestroika and its notions of social democratization also may have cut mortality rates by inspiring hopes for a better future (Notzon et al., 1998).

Suicides decreased and mortality rates fell during this period despite casualties from the war in Afghanistan.[2]

Some of the increase in mortality in the late 1980s is apparently due to the abandonment of the antialcohol campaign and may be attributed to deaths that the campaign "postponed." That is, many of the persons most susceptible to dying from alcohol-related causes did not do so during the course of the campaign; rather, their deaths were "postponed" until its cessation. Islamic areas of Russia and the former Soviet Union saw less fluctuation in their rates of death attributable to alcohol because of their lower levels of alcohol consumption (Treml, 1997; Shkolnikov et al., 1998).[3] This gives further credibility to the presumption that the antialcohol campaign played an important role in cutting mortality in the mid-1980s.

Working-age mortality for both men and women increased sharply following the breakup of the Soviet Union in the early 1990s. The regions most affected were the urban and most economically developed areas of European Russia, which had high rates of labor turnover, large increases in reported crime, and more unequal distributions of household income (Leon and Shkolnikov, 1998; Walberg et al., 1998). This suggests that social stress played a role in increasing mortality, particularly for deaths by such causes as circulatory diseases, injuries from accidents and other trauma, poisoning, and violence.

CHANGING CAUSES OF WORKING-AGE MALE MORTALITY

Analysis of the changes in Russian mortality by age and sex depicted in Figure 4.3 showed that increases in Russian working-age male

---

[2] Between 1984 and 1996, the suicide rate fell by about 40 percent, while the homicide rate fell more than 30 percent (Meslé et al., 1996). For more on the decline in deaths by injury, poisoning, or violence during the antialcohol campaign, see Shkolnikov, Meslé, and Vallin (1997).

[3] Islamic areas still enjoy lower mortality and higher life expectancy than other areas of the Russian Federation. Death rates in areas with the highest concentrations of Islamic religious communities are lower than they are elsewhere in Russia. Working-age male mortality for all but one of these areas is also lower than that for Russia as a whole. See Krindatch (1996) for oblast-level data on Islamic religious community concentration and Pashintseva, Voronina, and Kazachenko (1998) for oblast-level mortality data.

mortality are most responsible for changes in life expectancy. Further analysis of changes in male life expectancy by cause of death helps identify the reasons for changing health and mortality conditions since 1984 (Figure 4.5).

Male life expectancy has fluctuated widely in the past two decades, as have the reasons for changing life expectancy. Changes in deaths by external causes, i.e., those caused by injuries, poisoning, and violence, have effected great changes in life expectancy since 1984, and changes in deaths from circulatory diseases have effected great changes in life expectancy in the 1990s.

Changes in the causes of death since 1984, and subsequent changes in life expectancy, illustrate changing Russian health problems in the past two decades. We consider four subperiods:

- From 1984 to 1987, the period of the antialcohol campaign, when male life expectancy increased by more than three years
- From 1987 to 1992, the period following the abandonment of the campaign, during which male life expectancy decreased by nearly three years
- From 1992 to 1994, the period following the dissolution of the Soviet Union, when male life expectancy decreased by four and a half years, reaching its lowest level in four decades in 1994
- From 1994 to 1996, when male life expectancy increased by over two years[4]

[4] Data on the contributions since 1996 of changes in cause of death to changes in life expectancy are not available. Although the latest decline in life expectancy is too recent for us to analyze all the reasons for it, Popov (2001) suggests that, while the economy grew and unemployment declined after the August 1998 currency crisis, a decline in real incomes led to social stress causing increased mortality and lower life expectancy.

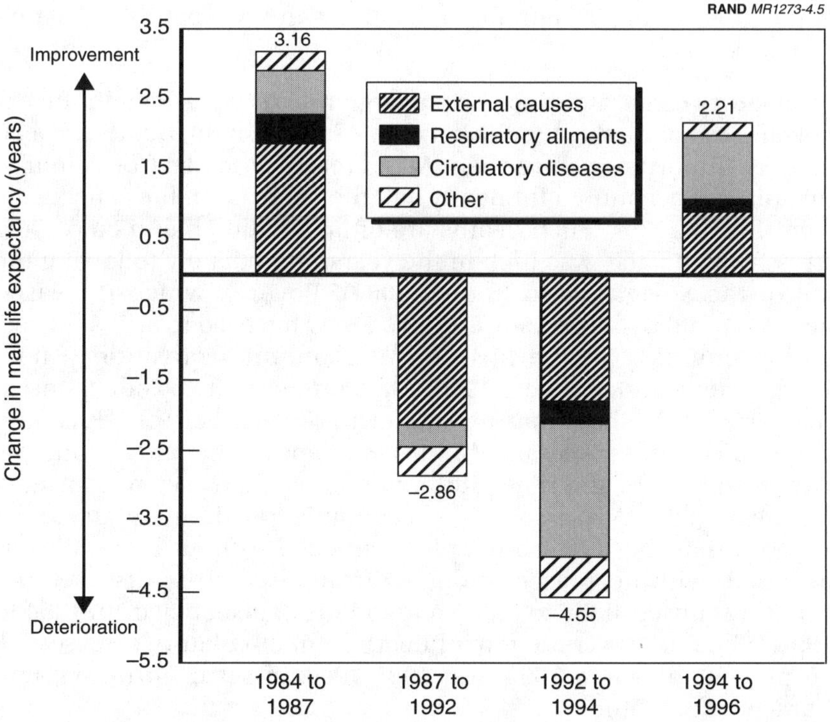

SOURCES: Shkolnikov and Meslé (1996); Shkolnikov (1997); Shkolnikov (1998).

Figure 4.5—Contribution of Different Causes of Death to Changes in Russian Male Life Expectancy, 1984–96

Most of the increase in life expectancy from 1984 to 1987 was attributable to a decline in deaths from external causes. Nearly all the decrease in life expectancy from 1987 to 1992 is attributable to increases in deaths from external causes, often linked to consequences of alcohol and alcoholism. A particularly telling indicator of the effect of alcohol on Russian health is the rate of death from alcohol poisoning. Russian deaths per 100,000 population from accidental alcohol poisoning have fluctuated from 19.6 in 1984 just before the antialcohol campaign to 7.8 in 1988 as the antialcohol campaign was ending to 37.4 in 1994, or about 200 times the comparable U.S. rate (Treml, 1997).

Circulatory disease did not play a large role in variations in life expectancies before the dissolution of the Soviet Union, but it has been of great importance since then. An increase in deaths from circulatory disease accounted for nearly half the decrease in life expectancy from 1992 to 1994. Such deaths are often attributable to emotional stress, which likely was high in the years immediately following the fall of the Soviet Union (Stone, 2000). Poverty, which increased nearly 20-fold between 1987 and 1993, may have led to stress exacerbating mortality in the post-Soviet economic transition (Chen, Wittgenstein, and McKeon, 1996). Data on mortality by education in the early 1990s show that persons with lower levels of education, and, hence, perhaps lesser abilities to adapt to changing economic circumstances of the time, suffered greater increases in mortality (Andreev, 1999). As the social and economic transition progressed, it appears that the Russian people reconciled to it and stress levels declined, with decreases in deaths from circulatory disease contributing substantially to an increase in life expectancy from 1994 to 1996.[5] Overall, the crude rate of death from circulatory diseases fell 10 percent between 1994 and 1997 (Pashintseva, Voronina, and Kazachenko, 1998).

Respiratory diseases and other causes of death, including cancer, are not important in explaining variations in Russian male life expectancy in the past two decades. Nevertheless, it is important to note that the rates of death from these and virtually every other cause in Russia are unacceptably high. Rates of death by most major causes are higher for Russian working-age men than for their American counterparts (Figure 4.6).

---

[5] To be sure, the adaptation is a continuing process, but it shows signs of progressing. In July 1999, only 32 percent of Russians claimed that their family had adapted "to the changes that happened in the country during the last ten years," while 45 percent claimed that their families "shall never adapt." By November 2000, 48 percent claimed that their families had adapted, and only 29 percent said their families would never adapt (Russian Center for Public Opinion and Market Research, 2000).

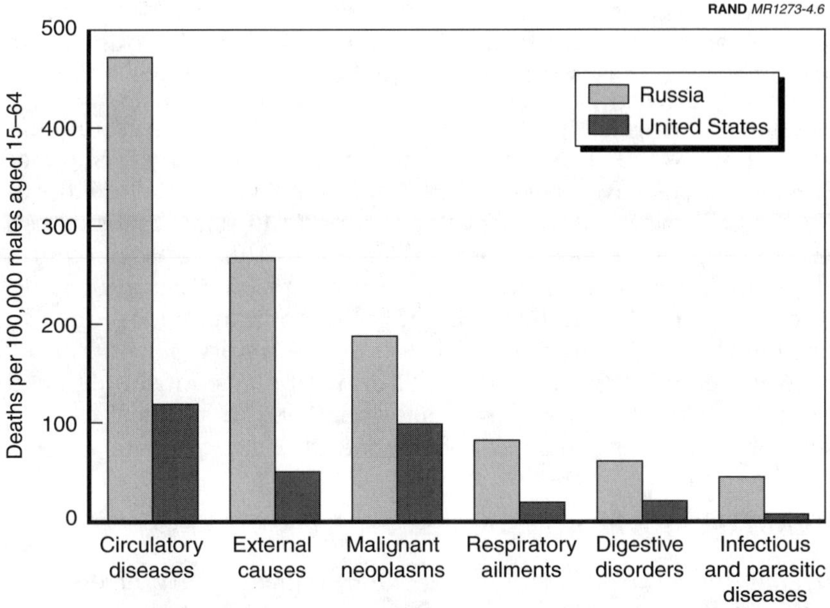

SOURCE: World Health Organization (1998).

Figure 4.6—Rates of Death by Leading Causes for Males Aged 15–64 in Russia and the United States, 1994–95

Overall, Russian working-age males have a death rate about four times that for U.S. males of the same age group.[6] Russian males of working age die from external causes such as injuries, accidents, poisoning, homicide, and suicide at nearly six times the rate U.S. males do. Their rates of death from infectious and parasitic diseases, many preventable or treatable, are five times those for U.S. males. High rates of infectious or parasitic disease, such as tuberculosis, often

---

[6] Although data on deaths by cause by age and sex are available for both the Russian Federation and the United States through 1997, *comparable* data are currently available only through 1995. There are some minor differences in statistics on deaths by cause between the Russian Federation and the United States making impossible exact comparisons of deaths by cause by age and sex since 1995. In 1997, statistics on all deaths indicate there were 1,160 deaths for every 100,000 males 15 to 64 years old in Russia, but only 392 deaths for every 100,000 males 15 to 64 in the United States (Pashintseva, Voronina, and Kazachenko, 1998; Hoyert, Kochanek, and Murphy, 1999).

indicate a less advanced health system. Russian deaths from circulatory diseases are about three times higher and those from cancers and digestive diseases are about twice those for U.S. males.

Russian working-age males suffer death rates from respiratory diseases that are four times higher than those suffered by U.S. males. Smoking likely plays a role in the higher rate of respiratory deaths for Russian males. Smoking prevalence among Russian males is estimated to have increased from 53 percent in 1985 to 67 percent in 1992 and remains more than twice the rate for U.S. adult males (Prokhorov, 1997).[7] Higher levels of pollution in Russia also may account for the higher number of deaths by respiratory causes there. As we will see, however, while the environment may contribute to high mortality rates in the Russian Federation, it does not appear to be responsible for recent changes in those rates.

HEALTH CARE IN RUSSIA

Overall Russian trends in life expectancy reflect in part the development, and then the stagnation, of the Soviet and Russian health care systems (Eberstadt, 1990). At its origin the Soviet health system had to address problems for a population whose life expectancy, then only about 40 years, would be among the lowest in the world today, or comparable to that in contemporary Angola, Ethiopia, Malawi, and Mozambique. It sought to bring communicable and infectious diseases under control through a labor-intensive system with low treatment costs. It largely succeeded in doing so, as the life expectancy figures attest. Such a system, emphasizing quantity over quality, did not require highly trained personnel, and the Soviet system made extensive use of personnel with only brief medical or public health training.

---

[7] Smoking prevalence among U.S. adult males declined from 33 percent in 1985 to 28 percent in 1990 and to 27 percent in 1995 (U.S. Census Bureau, 1999). The Russia Longitudinal Monitoring Survey (RLMS) shows a somewhat lower rate of smoking for Russian males in 1992 (60 percent) than that cited by Prokhorov (1997) but no significant change since then (Zohoori et al., 1999). The RLMS also shows Russian adult males to have smoking rates at least six times those for Russian women, although smoking rates for Russian women have increased by nearly half in recent years. As a result, per capita consumption of cigarettes in Russia has increased by nearly a third since 1994 (World Health Organization, 2000c).

The overall characteristics of such a system can become weaknesses when health needs change. The progress of the Soviet health system stalled after bringing major infectious diseases under control (Andreev, 1999). By 1965, the Soviet health system appears to have made nearly as much progress as it could against the diseases it was designed to combat. New health problems were confronting the nation; specifically, "civilization" diseases, such as cancer, cardiovascular disease, and those resulting from alcohol and tobacco use, were becoming more prominent. Unlike health care systems in the West, the Russian health care system has been unable to enter the next phase of mortality reduction and health care improvement, in which the negative effects of industrialization are overcome through measures to improve living and working conditions as well as health education. Hence, Russian life expectancy has stagnated in recent decades while that in the West and in other advanced nations continues to improve.

Trends in age-specific death rates since World War II underscore the achievements, and current problems, of the Russian health care system. While mortality rates for infants and young children are small fractions of what they were in the late 1940s and early 1950s, those for working-age males are nearly identical now to what they were then.[8] The improvement in infant and child mortality coupled with increasing overall mortality underscores the role of increasing working-age mortality in increasing Russian death rates.

Previously centralized health planning has led to inefficient health care investments in training and equipment (Bloom and Malaney, 1998). Over time, the Soviet health system has sought to produce more medical professionals with very narrow specializations, giving the system a pronounced vertical character. Soviet physicians chose

---

[8] While overall mortality rates have increased in the past two years, infant mortality has continued to decline; provisional figures show only 15.8 infants per thousand died in 2000, compared with 16.4 in 1999 (Agence France Presse, 2001a). We note that historical trends on mortality and life expectancy in Russia are available only through considerable efforts by demographers seeking to reconstruct mortality data that were not always forthcoming from Soviet authorities. Readers wishing to know more about Soviet and Russian statistics on mortality, their compilation and publication, and possible distortions in them (such as those resulting from efforts to reconcile the pre-1993 definition of infant mortality in Russia with that used elsewhere in the world) should consult, inter alia, Meslé et al. (1996), Anderson and Silver (1997), and Andreev (1999).

a narrow specialty at the beginning of their training, with specialties such as those based on age of patient or a particular diagnostic or surgical procedure (Twigg, 2000). This led to such anomalies as heart specialists unable to perform heart surgery and to extensive use of referrals to other professionals for further procedures or diagnoses.[9]

Beyond the problems of overspecialization, the Soviet health system has produced, as the American health system once did, too few health professionals, such as general and nurse practitioners, who could provide general preventive rather than specialized curative care. The most recent comparable statistics on medical professionals show Russia to have nearly 55 percent more physicians per capita than the United States, but 25 percent fewer nurses (World Health Organization, 2000b). The Russian ratio of physicians to population has grown nearly 10 percent since 1992, while the Russian ratio of nurses to population has declined slightly (World Health Organization, 2000c). The concentration of physicians and nurses working in hospitals has increased slightly, while the percentage of general practitioners in primary health care has declined. There are nearly ten times as many physicians in hospitals as there are in primary health care establishments away from hospitals. The growing population of medical professionals is poorly paid. Unlike U.S. physicians, who earn salaries well above the national average, Russian medical professionals earn salaries below the national average; the most qualified physicians thus have incentive to leave Russia (Naumova, 1998).[10]

While the Soviet health system did succeed in controlling infectious and contagious diseases to the point that it brought life expectancy

[9] The narrow specialization of Soviet physicians also may have helped limit broader medical knowledge. A former Soviet health minister once complained that Russian physicians graduated from medical school without knowing how to take blood pressure readings (Goldberg, 2000a). In fact, almost half of a 1990 Soviet medical school graduating class could not read an electrocardiogram on the day they got their diplomas (Specter, 1995). When confronted with new diseases or medicines, some Soviet and Russian physicians, rather than turning to laboratory experimentation, would prescribe new medicines and see how they worked on patients (Garrett, 2000).

[10] In the mid-1990s, Russian doctors were earning about $145 per month, less than drivers or baby-sitters (Specter, 1995). More generally, Twigg (2001) notes, "health care is disastrously underfunded in Russia" because "the Russian government, from the federal to municipal levels, routinely fails or refuses to provide legally mandated health benefits."

very close to Western levels in the 1960s, it appears that the present health care system has been losing its ability to do so. The political, social, and economic changes of the 1990s have devastated what was an extensive health care system and infrastructure delivering free and accessible health care to all, albeit health care sometimes of questionable quality. One Russian health care official observed that changes in the health care system "have mostly destroyed what existed before, and nothing has replaced it" (Wines and Zuger, 2000).[11]

Resurgence of Russian Tuberculosis

Recent difficulties Russia has had combating tuberculosis illustrate problems the health care system has both in combating disease and in modernizing practices. Worldwide, tuberculosis is a bigger killer than either malaria or AIDS, killing more persons than any other infectious disease (Grange and Zumla, 1999). Its recent increase in Russia illustrates the problems Russia faces from the economic turmoil and social upheaval it has experienced in the 1990s. Tuberculosis rates in Russia are above those in China, Brazil, and Mexico, three times those seen elsewhere in Europe, and about ten times those in the United States and Canada (Figure 4.7).

Prior to the Soviet revolution in 1917, Russia had one of the highest rates of tuberculosis in Europe and hardly any state policy to combat it (Farmer et al., 1999). During World War I, the number of Russian deaths caused by tuberculosis, 2 million, exceeded the number of Russian soldiers killed by the war, 1.7 million. At that time, there were only 18 sanatoria and fewer than 1,000 beds dedicated to tuberculosis patients. The control of tuberculosis became one of the top priorities of the Soviet government, and one to which the Soviet authorities devoted considerable resources. By the time of World War II, the Soviet Union had more than 100,000 beds available to tuber-

[11]Wines and Zuger (2000) note that "since 1990, Russia has decentralized its Soviet health bureaucracy, then tried to recentralize it; thrown the door open to private insurers, then moved to close it; guaranteed free medicine to those who needed it, then limited free medicine to the neediest. Eight different health ministers have tried to run the system during the last 10 years."

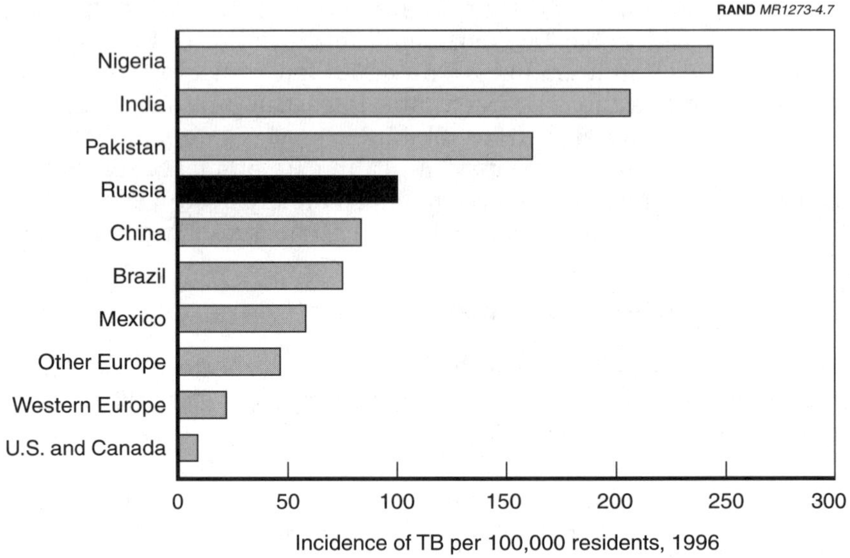

SOURCE: Netto et al. (1998).

Figure 4.7—Tuberculosis Rates in Russia and Some Other Nations and Regions

culosis patients and more than 3,800 specialists trained to serve them, with 18 tuberculosis research centers to seek further advances against the disease. There were periodic reversals in the Soviet battle against tuberculosis, but by 1960 progress had advanced to the point that Soviet authorities were predicting the eventual eradication of the disease in Russia. While rates of death from other causes were rising, tuberculosis death rates declined by two-thirds between the mid-1960s and the late 1980s (Figure 4.8).

In the 1990s, worsening social and economic conditions, subsequent declines in living standards, and an increase in the number of persons without permanent homes or jobs contributed to increases in tuberculosis. In the early 1990s the tuberculosis death rate nearly

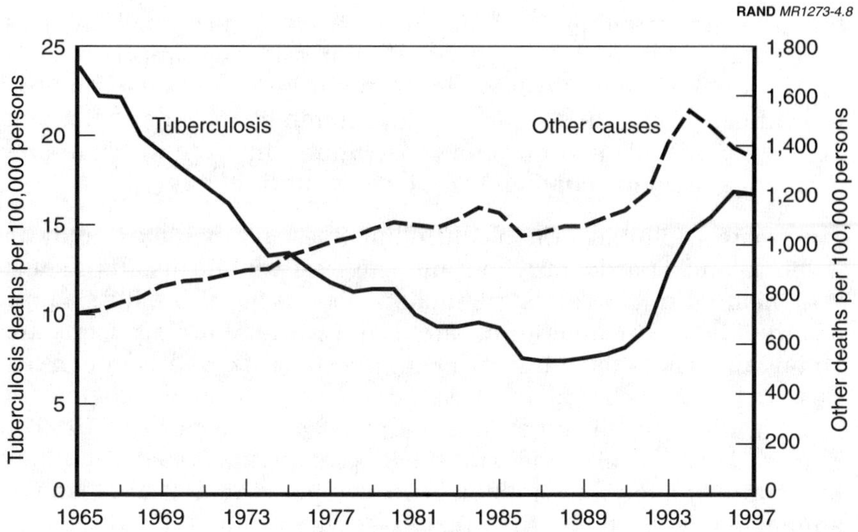

SOURCES: Meslé at al. (1996); Pashintseva et al. (1998).

Figure 4.8—Russian Rates of Death from Tuberculosis and All Other Causes, 1965–97

doubled; by the late 1990s, it reached levels not seen in Russia since the early 1970s.[12]

Recurring, or recrudescent, tuberculosis in Russia presents several challenges for a health system that cannot handle it without help. Russia and the other states of the former Soviet Union are the site of the first widespread tuberculosis recrudescence within Europe in the past century (Farmer et al., 1999). Unfortunately, because most cases of widespread tuberculosis are in developing nations, no one has designed a single effective program to treat increasing prevalence of

---

[12] Preliminary reports for 2000 indicate the mortality rate from tuberculosis now exceeds 20 per 100,000 inhabitants, its highest level since the late 1960s (Agence France Presse, 2001b). Three in four tuberculosis victims in 2000 were working-age adults. Overall incidence is 90 per 100,000 persons, with incidence in Russian prisons exceeding 3,100 per 100,000 persons.

tuberculosis among patients in nations with "civilization" diseases such as alcoholism and drug addiction or with high imprisonment rates. Russian tuberculosis patients might be better served by the individualized treatment traditionally offered by Soviet and Russian medicine, but this regimen now costs more than the Russian government and many individual Russians can afford.[13]

The greatest complication in controlling Russian tuberculosis may be its prevalence, particularly in multidrug-resistant forms, in prisons. With nearly 1 million of its 145 million persons in prison, Russia now has the highest incarceration rate in the world, and its prisons are among the places most infected with tuberculosis. Nearly one in ten Russian prisoners has active tuberculosis; of these, nearly 20 percent have multidrug-resistant strains of the disease (Farmer et al., 1999). The head of medical services for the Russian prison system estimates that approximately $400 million is needed per year, or more than the annual budget for the entire prison system, to combat the disease in Russian prisons (Uzelac, 2000a).[14]

Faced with growing incidence of the disease, increased prevalence of its multidrug-resistant strains, and limited recourses, Russian and international health officials have worked to develop more cost-efficient programs to treat it.[15] The high rates of tuberculosis in Russia present a direct threat to the international community: drug-resistant tuberculosis cases have been reported among travelers

---

[13] The World Health Organization recommends a Directly Observed Therapy Shortcourse of treatments (DOTS), a low-cost method to treat tuberculosis, but Russia traditionally has treated the disease through more individualized, and more expensive, treatment. The DOTS was developed chiefly for the control of tuberculosis in developing regions, where poverty and undernutrition complicate treatment. While helpful in treating tuberculosis in Russia, it has not succeeded as well there as it has elsewhere. Traditional Soviet and Russian methods of treating tuberculosis are about three times more expensive per patient than is the DOTS (Farmer et al., 1999; Uzelac, 2000a).

[14] Money is needed for treating both inmates in jail and those who have been released. Each year about 30,000 prisoners with active tuberculosis are released from Russian prisons, with many of these failing to continue treatment after their release (Farmer et al., 1999).

[15] A "DOTS-Plus" program, for example, seeks to provide both greater efficacy and efficiency in treating tuberculosis among Russian patients (Farmer et al., 1999).

from the former Soviet Union to the United States (Farmer et al., 1999).[16]

The Growth of HIV/AIDS in Russia

Increasing rates of tuberculosis may complicate Russian efforts to deal with a growing number of HIV and AIDS cases. Infection by *mycobacterium tuberculosis* leads to tuberculosis among only one in ten infected, but it is much more likely to lead to the disease among those also infected with HIV (Ravglione et al., 1996). This is especially problematic in Russian prisons which, in addition to high rates of tuberculosis, also appear to have high rates of HIV infection (Powell, 2000). Furthermore, Russians now contracting tuberculosis are more than three times as likely to die from the disease as they were in 1985 (Feshbach, 2001).

Among the entire Russian population, HIV/AIDS rates appear to be growing rapidly. Russia suffered less than 1,000 AIDS deaths in 1999, but estimates of the current Russian population living with HIV or AIDS range from 130,000 to 500,000 to still more (UNAIDS, 2000; Piper, 1999; Krupenik, 2001; Feshbach, 2001).The current HIV population is concentrated in or near Moscow, Saint Petersburg, and the Irkutsk region, as well as among men and those 20 to 30 years of age (Bazhenova, 2001b). By comparison, in 1999, there were 20,000 deaths from AIDS and 850,000 persons living with HIV/AIDS in the United States (UNAIDS, 2000). Vadim Pokrovsky, the Chief of the Russian Center for the Prevention of AIDS, estimates that, by the end of 2001, there may be more than one million persons with HIV in Russia (Bazhenova, 2001b). In 2000, the number of HIV carriers and AIDS patients is estimated to have increased fourfold (Interfax, 2001).[17]

---

[16] Some health experts worry that, if infectious diseases continue to rise in Russia, the country could become an "epidemiologic pump," spreading infectious diseases elsewhere in the world (Zuger, 2000).

[17] One possible indicator of future increases in HIV infection, and potential to control them, is the incidence of other sexually transmitted diseases. Between 1990 and 1997 the incidence of syphilis increased 50 times, to 278 per 100,000 persons, but reported statistics show a substantial decline from 1997 to 1999, to 188 per 100,000 persons (World Health Organization, 2000c).

Intravenous drug use has caused rapid spread of the disease among Russians. The mid-1990s saw both an increase and change in the number of HIV infections by source in Russia (MacWilliam, 1997). Between 1987 and 1995, about half of the HIV cases registered with health officials were attributable to sexual contact. In 1996, however, more than three in five new HIV cases were attributed to intravenous drug use. A 1999 outbreak of HIV among intravenous drug users in Moscow "resulted in the reporting of more than three times as many new HIV cases that year than in all previous years combined" (UNAIDS, 2000). Intravenous drug use has also led to sharp rises in HIV and AIDS elsewhere in Russia (United Press International, 2000; Wines, 2000a).

Much of the Soviet and later Russian response to AIDS has reflected the ideology of Soviet medicine and the later problems in Russian health care. Original Soviet efforts against the disease featured an emphasis on quantitative indicators, with mass screenings of 140 million persons identifying 774 persons (or about 1 in 200,000) with HIV infection (Powell, 2000). Today most Russian hospitals lack the funds for AIDS drugs or equipment commonly available in the West.[18]

Conclusion

Improvements in the Russian health system may, if implemented, lead to improvements in Russian health care and reduce mortality rates for all Russians. Many such improvements, however, will require many years to implement, and still more years to have an effect. Furthermore, deterioration in the Russian health system cannot adequately explain the most distinct problem of Russian health in the past few years—that of high mortality for working-age males. Therefore, even if it could be done quickly, health care system improvement would not necessarily help cut mortality among a population that suffers from behavioral health risks (e.g., smoking and

---

[18] Powell (2000), for example, notes that protease inhibitors must be obtained at Western clinics. While Russia has an adequate supply of azidotimidine, there is a shortage of other drugs used to treat AIDS-related infections. Western nations use disposable hypodermics to control the spread of AIDS but cost constraints often force Russian physicians to reuse disposable equipment. The alcohol used to sterilize nondisposable equipment is often in short supply because it is frequently imbibed.

drinking) that cannot be treated effectively by acute care. We therefore turn to other explanations for recent fluctuations in and high levels of mortality for the population for whom it has changed most: working-age males.

EXPLANATIONS FOR RECENT TRENDS IN RUSSIAN WORKING-AGE MORTALITY

Both the high levels of and fluctuations in Russian mortality in the past decade have drawn considerable attention, which has led to speculation on their possible causes. In addition to the deterioration of the health care system, the other most popular explanations are environmental conditions, varying levels of alcohol consumption, and social and economic change. We discuss each of these below.

Environment

The Russian environment is certainly troubled after years of reckless treatment by the Soviets, and may well be a contributor to high rates of death from respiratory and other ailments in Russia that we have seen. The rate at which Russian industry releases toxic metals such as arsenic and lead into the air is several hundred, and sometimes several thousand, times that of industry in the European Economic Community (Feshbach, 1995). In the early 1990s, according to government monitoring, concentrations of phenols and petroleum products in Russian rivers—the source of drinking water for most of the population—often exceeded ambient water quality standards by a factor of two to ten times (Peterson, 1993). Some Russian researchers have estimated that half the population uses drinking water falling below microbiologic and chemical standards for public health (Tuchinsky and Varavikova, 1996).

While such extreme conditions undoubtedly contribute to the high levels of mortality and adversely affect the health of Russians, they cannot explain recent mortality differentials and trends. Environmental conditions should affect all persons equally, but mortality has increased much more for males than females. Changes in environmental conditions cannot explain why recent changes in mortality have been greatest for persons in their prime ages rather than among the more vulnerable young and old. If environmental conditions were behind recent mortality trends, we would expect changes in deaths caused by cancer or respiratory ailments to be even more pronounced. Finally, the decline and fall of the Soviet system had an immediate environmental benefit. Industrial emissions fell in the late 1980s and early 1990s as state-run factories floundered, yet this is the period when mortality rates increased the most (Stone, 2000).

Alcohol

Some have suggested that varying levels of alcohol consumption have contributed to variations in Russian working-age mortality, especially for working-age males. There is considerable evidence for this. We have already seen how rates of death, especially for external causes such as accidents and violence often related to alcohol use, decreased for working-age males during the antialcohol campaign and increased after its cessation. We also noted earlier that Islamic areas saw less fluctuation in their rates of death attributable to alcohol because of their lower levels of alcohol consumption. In this subsection, we explore further the relationship of trends in mortality rates and life expectancy to trends and patterns of alcohol consumption.

Russian male life expectancy reached its highest levels ever shortly after per capita alcohol consumption dropped sharply in the mid-1980s (Figure 4.9). When alcohol consumption increased in the late 1980s and early 1990s, life expectancy for all males plunged to nearly 57 years of age (Figure 4.10). Alcohol consumption increased most among those most affected by the economic crisis of the time, low-income males (Zohoori et al., 1998). Since peaking in 1993, alcohol consumption has declined again. Per capita alcohol consumption for adult Russian males in 1998 was a third less than its level in 1993, and life expectancy for all males was nearly four years higher in 1998 than it had been five years earlier.

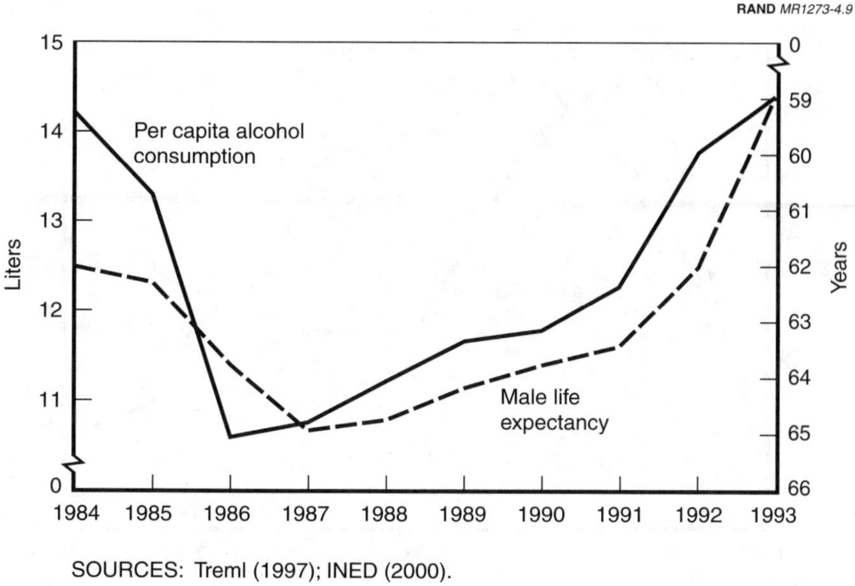

Figure 4.9—Total Alcohol Consumption and Russian Male Life Expectancy, 1984–93 (note inverted scale for life expectancy)

Russians still have a very high level of alcohol consumption. Russian per capita alcohol consumption exceeds the level that the World Health Organization says endangers health in a country (Uzelac, 2000b). The Russian style of drinking contributes to its dangers. Traditionally, "holiday-peak" drinking predominated in Russia, with imbibers drinking large quantities during short periods on Sundays or church holidays (Shkolnikov and Nemtsov, 1997). Russia was a highly agrarian society when this pattern developed, and alcohol consumption was low during other times of the week or year. Binge drinking plays a disproportionate role in recent Russian mortality, with sudden deaths from alcohol poisoning, accidents, and violence highest during weekends (Chenet et al., 1998).

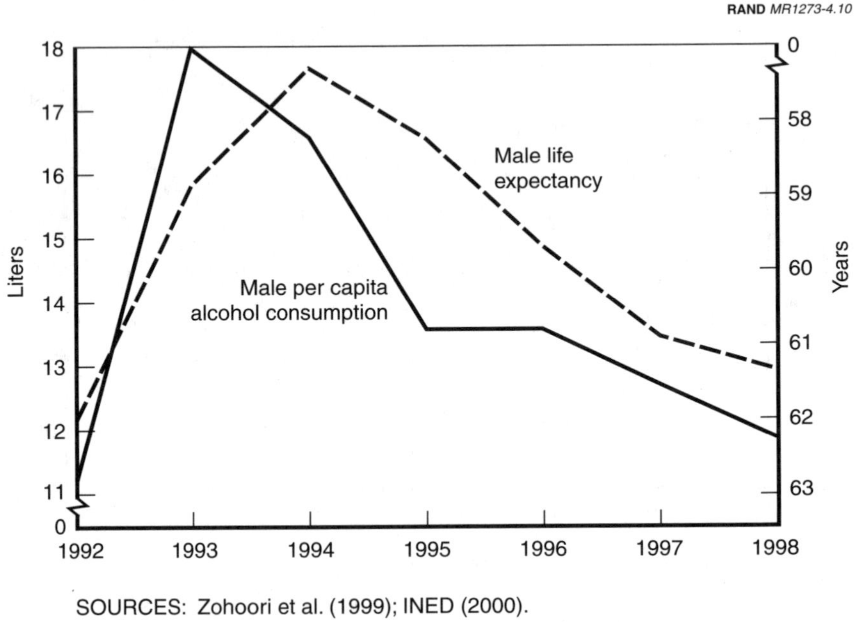

Figure 4.10—Alcohol Consumption and Life Expectancy for Russian Males, 1992–98 (note inverted scale for life expectancy)[19]

Russian preferences in alcoholic beverages also contribute to deaths caused by alcohol consumption. Vodka has long been the alcoholic drink of choice among Russians, and the drinking of large quantities of vodka with little food often results in deaths by accident and violence (Shkolnikov and Nemtsov, 1997). France and Italy in the 1970s had per capita consumption of alcohol similar to that in Russia today but, because most of their alcohol consumption was of wine, it did

[19] Statistics on per capita alcohol consumption in Figure 4.9 are not comparable with those in Figure 4.10. Figure 4.9 shows per capita alcohol consumption for the total population as calculated from estimates of state-produced and homemade alcoholic beverages. Figure 4.10 shows per capita alcohol consumption for adult males only as calculated from self-reports by respondents to the Russia Longitudinal Monitoring Survey.

not lead to high rates of violence or accidental deaths (Medvedev, 1996).[20]

The antialcohol campaign and subsequent state policy appears to have affected Russian tastes, with alcohol restrictions leading Russians to seek more potent drinks, legal or otherwise. One estimate (Treml, 1997) shows vodka consumption increasing from 53 percent of total legal alcohol consumption in 1985 to 81 percent in 1993, while official statistics on alcohol sales show sales of "vodka and liqueurs" increasing 22 percent between 1993 and 1998 (RF Goskomstat, 1999c). Even after the antialcohol campaign ended, per capita consumption of samogon, or illegal homemade alcohol, increased, while that of alcohol sold by the state remained at levels from before the campaign (Treml, 1997). The poor quality of much samogon may contribute to alcohol-related deaths. Autopsy reports show a high number of deaths from alcohol poisoning result not from the concentration of alcohol per se but from high concentrations of toxins in the alcohol (Shkolnikov and Nemtsov, 1997). Government easing of laws on the production and sale of liquor also appears to have helped increase the availability and consumption of alcohol, leading to a reduction of its price in real terms when alcohol consumption was at its peak (Medvedev, 1996; Shkolnikov and Meslé, 1996).

Social and Economic Change

Much of the variation in alcohol consumption, and the corresponding variation in mortality, appears to be attributable to social and economic change. Alcohol consumption was greatest in the early 1990s, shortly after the dissolution of the Soviet Union, when the pace of social and economic change was rapid. Social and economic changes have had both short-term and long-term effects on Russian health and mortality.

[20] Overall, Russian mortality from alcoholism is about one-fifth that of France and Italy, but mortality from accidental poisoning is negligible in France and high in Russia (Shkolnikov and Meslé, 1996). In other words, deaths from alcohol in France and Italy are more likely to be the result of chronic diseases such as cirrhosis of the liver, while deaths from alcohol in Russia are more likely to be the result of binges leading to sudden death.

As we have seen from trends over the past few decades, increases in Russian mortality, particularly for males, rather than resulting solely from recent economic crises, first started in the mid-1960s. This may have been the point at which not just the Soviet health system but the Soviet economic system more generally began to adversely affect the health of Russians through decisions ostensibly designed to increase wealth but having deleterious consequences for the health of Russians.

One example of this is in Soviet agricultural planning. During the 1960s, the Soviet government increased production, marketing, and consumption of meat and dairy products, with the Khruschev government specifically calling for the doubling of meat and dairy products and some reduction in potato and bread consumption (Popkin et al., 1997). This occurred as Soviet household income, thanks to rising petroleum prices, was increasing. The result was that the Russian diet became one of the richest in the world, with consumption of cereals and starches declining and that of sugar and red meat increasing. Such a diet can lead to increased mortality, particularly from coronary heart disease. As we saw earlier (Figure 4.6), Russian working-age males have rates of death from circulatory disease about three times higher than those prevalent for U.S. working-age males. In a way, we can say that Soviet agricultural policy and, ironically, prosperity of the 1960s probably contributed to the high rates of death from coronary heart disease three decades later.

Recent mortality trends appear to be more directly related to economic trends. Changes in Russian economic output have been drastic in the 1990s, and there appears to have been a strong correlation between life expectancy and performance of the economy. The sharp contraction of the economy saw the gross domestic product per capita decline from more than $6,300 in 1990 (as measured in 1998 U.S. dollars) to less than $3,600 in 1998. It may be that some Russians have been unable to take care of their own health and well-being in the deteriorating economic conditions of the 1990s, particularly as a market-oriented government replaced the paternalism of the Soviet government.

Chapter Five

DEMOGRAPHIC HISTORY, AGE STRUCTURE, AND FUTURE POLICY ISSUES

AGE AND SEX STRUCTURE OF THE RUSSIAN POPULATION

Russia's unique demographic history has produced a population with a unique age and sex structure. This demographic profile in turn raises special policy issues that Russia will have to confront now and in future years.

Demographers summarize the age and sex structure of a population through a population pyramid graph. This graph is called a "pyramid" because historically for most nations, particularly growing nations, it resembles a pyramid, with a wide base representing younger populations and a narrow top representing older populations closer to the end of their natural life span (see Figure 5.1).

The Russian population "pyramid" is hardly shaped like a pyramid (Figure 5.2). Its jagged "Christmas-tree" shape reflects the historical events that are shaping present and future demographics in Russia. Among these are a large imbalance of the population by sex and a very uneven distribution of the population by age. There are currently ten million more women than there are men in Russia. This is the largest such margin in the world (U.S. Census Bureau, 2000). It reflects in part the large number of male Russian casualties in World War II. Indeed, the imbalance of the population by sex is most evident at the top of the pyramid, for persons born before 1930.

The population imbalance by sex among persons born between 1930 and 1960 is somewhat smaller but still substantial. It reflects the higher mortality rates that Russian working-age men have suffered in recent years. Two other events of Russian demographic history are also evident in the graph for persons born between 1930 and 1960. First, there are very few Russians now in their mid-50s; this is because birth rates were very low during World War II. Second, there is a large number of Russians who were born after World War II, particularly in the 1950s, who will soon be approaching old age.

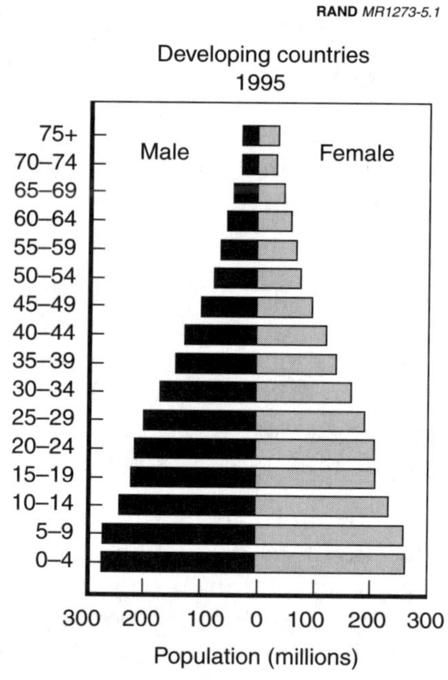

SOURCE: Bulatao (1998).

Figure 5.1—Typical Population Pyramid

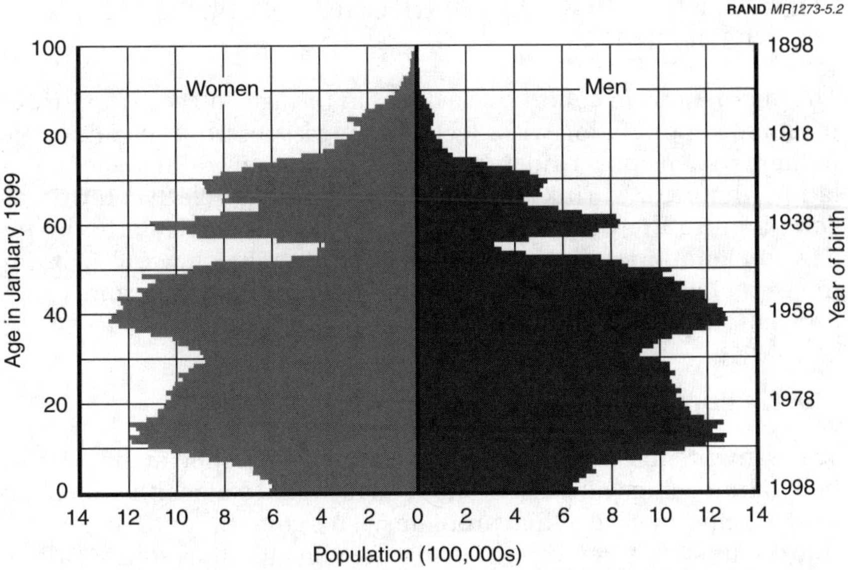

SOURCE: INED (2000).

Figure 5.2—Russian Population "Pyramid"

Growing urbanization in the 1960s led to declining birth rates and declining sizes of birth cohorts. During the 1960s the number of Russians born each year was less than the number born in the previous year. This changed in 1969, as the cohorts born shortly after World War II reached childbearing age. Birth cohorts generally increased in size until the late 1980s, reaching a peak of 2.5 million for those born in 1987. Since 1989, the number of Russians born each year generally has been less than the number born in the previous year.

It may be that the pronatalist incentives of the 1980s, launched in part over concern about declining population growth, helped accelerate population increases that population momentum alone would have accomplished. Declines in size of the youth population may accelerate future declines in the number of births. In 15 years, there will be half as many persons entering adulthood as there are today.

POLICY IMPLICATIONS OF THE CURRENT POPULATION AGE STRUCTURE

The fluctuations in cohort size evident in the age and sex structure of the Russian population will affect planning issues from schools to the military to pensions. Underlying these issues is a working-age population that will shrink in both absolute and relative terms as compared to the populations it must support, particularly the elderly. In addition to changes in the elderly population, we also examine expected changes in the working-age, military-age, and youth populations.

Elderly Population

The growth of the elderly population poses special problems. Population aging will present more challenges to a health system already facing myriad other problems. The government has few resources to strengthen the safety net for the elderly, and the elderly have few resources of their own from which they can draw. Many older persons during the Soviet era created wealth that never really existed or that was lost during the economic crises of the 1990s (Vassin, 1996).

Before the breakup of the USSR, Soviet pensions were near the average wage levels of the time, but during the 1990s Russian pension levels were between 30 and 40 percent of average wages, which also fell throughout the decade (Buckley, 2001). Pensions fell further in the year after the August 1998 currency crisis, with the average size of fixed monthly pensions declining by about a fourth in relation to the average monthly wage and by about a third in relation to the typical pensioner cost of living (RF Goskomstat, 1999c). As a result, Russia now faces a problem of widespread elderly poverty that barely existed before. Between August 1993 and October 1996, poverty rates increased greatly for persons of all ages, but especially for the elderly: poverty among persons of pension age increased tenfold, while that for the total population increased less than fourfold (Mroz, Mancini, and Popkin, 1999). Nevertheless, poverty among the elderly remains less severe than it is for others. The Russian Longitudinal Monitoring Survey shows that, while one in four persons of pension age lived in poverty in November 1998, the poverty rate for persons of pension age was below that of the general population, as well as that for another vulnerable age group—children six years of age or younger (Mroz, Mancini, and Popkin, 1999).

There are relatively more pension-age persons in Russia than elsewhere in the former Soviet Union (Buckley and Donahue, 2000). The Soviet pension system was a "pay-as-you-go" system, as the Russian system is today. Efforts to reform the pension system date from the late 1980s, but, after the collapse of the Soviet Union, such efforts were poorly synchronized with the economic reform efforts of the Russian government (Chandler, 2001). Supporting the pension system is more difficult for Russia alone than it would have been in association with other former Soviet states. Among former Soviet states outside the Baltics, Russia has the third highest percentage of population past pension age and the third lowest ratio of working-age to pension-age persons.[1] This means that each Russian worker bears a larger share of supporting the pension system than would be the case were the Soviet Union still extant. Expansions to the Soviet and subsequent Russian pension systems further constrain pension resources today. Less than half of all individuals past pension age were covered by the pension system in 1959; by 1997, coverage was nearly universal. In sum, the Russian pension system was designed for an age structure of a population in a nation that no longer exists, where population pressures would not have been as great, but whose pension mandates cannot now be changed easily.

Russia may face particularly acute problems in supporting its elderly when the large number of persons born in the 1950s leaves the workforce and is replaced by a much smaller number of persons born in the 1990s. Such problems might be overcome by increasing capital, and thereby productivity, per worker, but contraction of the Russian economy may prevent this option.

Russia may be able to learn some lessons from Western Europe in adjusting to growing numbers of older persons. The percent of the population 65 years of age or older is currently higher in Western

---

[1] Pension-age persons in the Soviet Union and Russian Federation are males past 59 years of age and females past 54 years of age. Unless otherwise noted, the discussion below on persons of pension age refers to persons of these ages, while discussions on persons of working age refer to males aged 15 to 59 and females aged 15 to 54.

Europe than in Russia, and is expected to grow more there (U.S. Census Bureau, 2000).[2] It is not clear if Russia will face the same demographic pressures in supporting its elderly population as nations in Western Europe and North America will face in supporting their elderly populations. Lengthening life spans in Europe and North America may create problems for financing government pensions. In Russia, it is possible that working-age mortality may be at such a level as to reduce future pension obligations without adversely affecting the ability of the nation to support current pension programs (Vishnevskii, 1999).

The oldest workers may face special problems in their last years of work. In the early 1990s, workforce participation declined more for workers 50 years of age or older than it did for other workers (Velkoff and Kinsella, 2000). The workforce participation rates of 25–49-year-old Russian workers is similar to that for U.S. workers of the same age, but those for older Russian workers not of pension age are lower than those for older U.S. workers (RF Goskomstat, 2000; U.S. Bureau of Labor Statistics, 2000). One possible explanation for lower workforce participation rates for older Russian workers is that some of them have been unable to adapt to the market economy or they have skills that are not in demand by the market economy (Williams, 1996). An analysis of workforce participation by elderly Russians shows it highest among more skilled and educated workers, with workforce participation among the best educated increasing in recent years (Gerber, 2001).

Working-Age Population

Despite high rates of working-age mortality in Russia, the working-age population has been growing for several years, and is projected to continue growing for several years more. This growth is due to two peculiarities in the age structure of the Russian population. Specifically, a very large number of youths born in the 1980s is or will soon be entering the workforce and replacing the small number of

---

[2] In Western Europe, persons 65 years of age or older comprise 16.3 percent of the population; in Russia, they comprise 12.6 percent (U.S. Census Bureau, 2000). The population 65 or older in Western Europe is projected to grow 32 percent by 2020, but only 19 percent in Russia.

persons born in the 1940s that is or will soon be retiring from the workforce. As a result, the Russian working-age population is expected to grow from less than 86 million in 1993 to more than 92 million in 2005. As a percent of the total population, the working-age population will increase from less than 58 percent to more than 64 percent. This growth in the working-age population means Russia has a demographic "window" to make changes needed for supporting a growing population of dependent ages, particularly of pension age. We discuss this further below in examining population dependency ratios.

Military-Age Population

Russia also faces planning problems from fluctuations in the size of its military-age population. The 15–24-year-old population is currently growing due to the large cohorts born in the 1980s, but, after peaking in 2004, it is projected to decline by nearly half by 2015 (U.S. Census Bureau, 2000). The relationship between population size and military and economic strength is more complex than traditional views hold, but population loss, coupled with a struggling economy, may weaken the Russian military.[3]

Many European states have experienced declines in their military-age populations, but they have been able to develop technologically sophisticated and capital-intensive forces to maintain their military strength, using either their own capital or sharing the burden of such efforts with their allies. Facing declining numbers of military-age youth and equipment problems for its forces, the Russian Defense Ministry plans to cut by the year 2005 the number of its military

---

[3] See Nichiporuk (2000) for a nuanced discussion of demographic factors and security dynamics. Many of the health problems affecting Russian society as a whole also may be affecting the Russian military and its fitness (Ball, 2000). Almost half of Russian draftees are unfit for service because of poor health. Russian military members, like other Russians, have also suffered from increased rates of infectious diseases such as tuberculosis and AIDS. Nevertheless, it is not entirely clear just how perilous these trends are for the Russian military (Zakharov, 2000a). Many Russian Federation youths, with the complicity of their parents and others, may be avoiding military service through bribes or other inducements to have their health declared too poor for military service. The resulting reliance by the military on poorer and more disadvantaged persons causes the health of Russian military members to be worse than it might be otherwise.

personnel to about three-fourths of current levels while increasing funding for better-equipped and better-trained units (Felgenhauer, 2000a).

Statistics on expenditures per member of the military (Taylor, 1999) help indicate how Russia fell behind other nations in developing capital-intensive forces. Between 1985 and 1998, while the total number of U.S. military personnel declined by more than a third, expenditures in real terms per member of the military increased by 11 percent (total U.S. defense spending in real terms declined 28 percent). Among all NATO nations of Europe combined, the total number of military personnel decreased by nearly a fourth, while expenditures per member of the military in real terms increased by 8 percent (total defense spending by these nations declined 17 percent). By contrast, Russia in 1998 was spending in real terms 15 percent less per member of its military than the USSR spent in 1985.[4]

Despite current plans to cut personnel so as to boost military spending per member, it is unclear to what extent Russia will be able to modernize its military. Its weak economy may prevent Russia from expending much capital on new military technology, and its peculiar position in the international community may prevent it from allying with wealthier nations for joint development of new military hardware and technology. At the same time, Russia may have trouble defending its huge land mass, as well as its more than 12,000 miles (20,000 km) of borders, should either defense planners, or demographic inevitabilities, indeed cut the number of military personnel. Such pressures may force Russia to rely on weapons of mass destruction, including nuclear weapons, for its security.[5]

---

[4] Comparative statistics on the number of military personnel in the Soviet Union in 1985 and in Russia today are not available.

[5] Recent Russian military doctrine on these topics has varied widely. In April 2000, Russian President Vladimir Putin approved a new military doctrine upgrading the role of nuclear weapons in Russian military strategy. The new doctrine envisages the possible first use of nuclear weapons by Russia to deter a mass attack by conventional forces (Reuters, 2000a). Yet by the end of 2000, Putin, in response to military leaders who advocated increases in conventional forces after NATO success against Serbia, had moved to cut Russian missile forces and increase resources for conventional forces (Felgenhauer, 2000b).

Youth Population

Fluctuations in youth populations also affect education planning. The Russian school-age population will soon decline as the cohorts born in the 1980s leave school and enter the workforce and the smaller cohorts born in the 1990s take their place. This means there will be less need for schools and teachers in coming years.[6] Yet it is also possible that the demand for schools and teachers will increase shortly thereafter, as persons born in the 1980s enter their childbearing years. This could cause an increase in the youth population through population momentum just as persons born in the 1950s helped boost the youth population in the 1970s, even in a time of declining fertility rates. In addition to raising a host of child-care issues, such fluctuations have economic implications for those who work with children—particularly women, who comprise disproportionate numbers of workers in health, education, and other social services (RF Goskomstat, 1999b).

Dependency Ratios

Some of the broad problems that Russia will face in supporting its young and old populations are reflected in expected changes in dependency ratios. Dependency ratios indicate the ratio of persons not of working age ("dependents") to those of working age (Figure 5.3).

The ratio of dependents to persons of working age has been declining in recent years and will continue to decline for several more years. Nearly all this decline in dependency ratios is attributable to a decline in the youth dependency ratio. In 1990, the youth

[6] The pending decline in school-age populations should temper proposals to manage the current shortage of teachers. The current bulge in school-age populations, caused in part by the large number of births in the 1980s, has led to a shortage of teachers. The most recent estimates are that Russia needs 50,000 more teachers for its schools. The Russian Minister of Education has proposed making "school service" a requirement for some university students (Karush, 2000). This may not be an ideal solution, but such temporary solutions may be more appropriate than any incentives to increase greatly the number of persons entering the teaching profession to educate what will soon be a rapidly declining number of students.

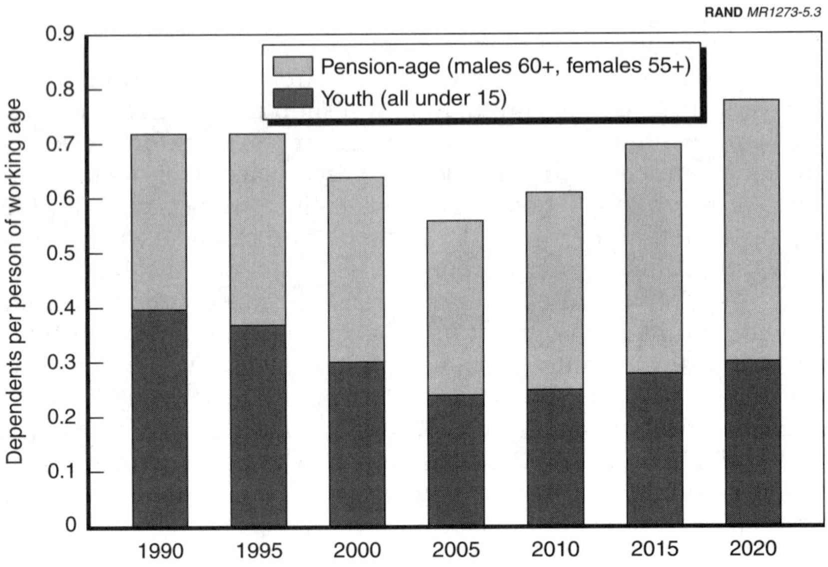

SOURCE: U.S. Census Bureau (2000).

Figure 5.3—Russian Dependency Ratios, 1990–2020[7]

dependency ratio—i.e., the ratio of persons less than 15 years old to those of working age—was 0.40. In 2000, it was 0.30, and by 2005 it will be 0.24. The youth dependency ratio is not expected to be as high as 0.30 again until 2020. By contrast, the pension-age dependency ratio, i.e., the ratio of persons of pension-age to those of working-age, has not changed much in the past decade, but it is expected to rise rapidly from 0.32 in 2005 to 0.48 in 2020.

The projected dependency ratios indicate that Russia will soon have to devote much more resources to its pension-age population and comparatively fewer to its youth population. The Russian pension-age population now exceeds the youth population. Still, the declining number of youths and the stable ratio of pension-age to working-age

[7] Again, "working-age" persons in Russia comprise males aged 15 to 59 and females aged 15 to 55. Males 60 and older and females 55 and older are eligible for state pensions.

persons give Russia a demographic "window" of opportunity in which it could plan for growing numbers of pension-age persons and for reallocating resources from youth to older populations. By 2010 this window will be closing, as both the youth and pension-age population will be growing faster than the working-age population.[8]

The challenge of supporting the growing population of pension age will vary greatly within Russia (Figure 5.4). Currently pension-age dependency ratios are lowest in the North, Far East, and Siberian regions, and highest in the Central and Black Soil regions of European Russia. More generally, regions with higher rates of natural increase

RANDMR1273-5.4.

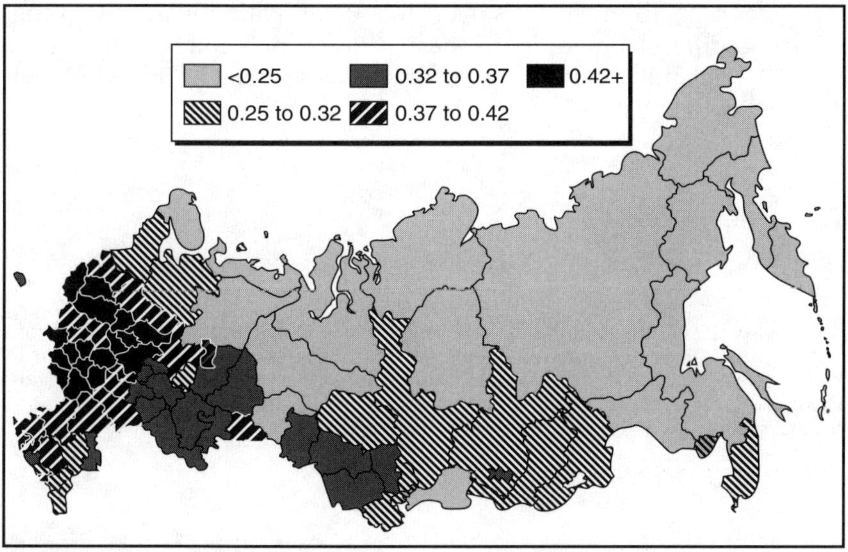

SOURCE: Pashintseva et al. (1998).

Figure 5.4—Pension-Age Dependency Ratio by Region, 1998

---

[8] We note, however, that projections of youth populations, and hence of youth dependency ratios, may be less accurate than projections of older populations. Projections of older populations in 2015 or 2020 are based on populations currently extant and on current mortality rates for this age group. Projections of youth populations rely on assumptions that may prove inaccurate about trends in fertility. For more on population forecasts and their accuracy by age group, see Bongaarts and Bulatao (2000).

have lower pension-age dependency ratios. This means that these regional differences may grow, because those regions with low pension-age dependency ratios are enjoying population growth, while those with high ratios are losing population. The concentration of pension-age persons in areas of higher population density may help Russia support this population, because older persons will be concentrated in areas where greater social infrastructure often accompanies higher population density.[9]

Population pyramids and projections help demographers and planners understand in advance the fluctuations that will occur in different age groups and the different services the population will need as its age composition changes over time. Even with advance warning, it can be difficult to adjust to these fluctuations. Such adjustments require a flexibility that has not characterized Soviet or Russian social services in the past.

---

9 Currently the elderly in some of these regions (e.g., Volga and Black Soil) are more likely to have pensions supporting them near or above subsistence level than others in Russia (Heleniak, 2001b). The federal nature of the Russian pension system means there are large regional disparities in pensions, with the elderly in some regions receiving pensions at less than three-fourths of subsistence level.

Chapter Six

WHAT CAN BE DONE TO ADDRESS DEMOGRAPHIC POLICY ISSUES IN RUSSIA?

What can be done to address policy issues arising from demographic trends in Russia? Several initiatives can alleviate conditions in the short term, but long-term problems will be more difficult to solve.

HEALTH CARE EDUCATION

Continuing improvements in contraceptive knowledge and access can help Russian women to lead more stable reproductive lives and avoid problems of maternal morbidity and mortality as well as secondary sterility arising from abortion. Increasing access to modern contraceptive methods in Russia appears to have helped reduce abortion rates. U.S. aid presently is seeking to fully develop the market for contraceptives in Russia, and hence further cut abortion rates, in part by making more information on a wider mix of contraceptives available to Russian women. Research from other countries indicates that better family planning services, including wider mixes of contraceptives, are especially important for preventing abortion where desired family size is small or declining (see, e.g., Rahman, DaVanzo, and Razzaque, forthcoming). Greater education on sexuality issues, both for Russian students and for Russian physicians, can yield benefits for all concerned, by helping the sexually active population avoid sexually transmitted diseases as well as the unstable and unhealthy pattern of reproductive behavior in which early childbirths are followed by subsequent abortions.

Broader public health education, similar to that undertaken in the United States, can help improve health behaviors. Russia has already initiated some efforts in this regard, such as including health warnings on tobacco advertisements similar to the warnings of the Surgeon General on U.S. advertisements of tobacco products. There are many other lessons from Western efforts to control tobacco consumption that Russia can apply, although their full development and impact, like that for most efforts to affect health behaviors, can take years to have a discernible effect on morbidity and mortality (Pierce, 1997).

More general lessons learned on public health education, such as instilling proper nutritional habits, can be applied to Russia from neighboring regions and nations. Finland in the 1970s faced many of the same health problems in cardiovascular diseases that Russia faces today. A health education program in North Karelia, a region bordering Russia that has few health care resources, helped improve dietary behaviors, cut tobacco consumption, decrease blood pressures, and increase physical activity among targeted males (Puska, 1997; Wines, 2000b). Although the situation in Russian Karelia is more dire—Finnish health officials sought to boost life expectancy, but Russian authorities first must stop its decline—Finnish, Russian, and Estonian officials have launched collaborative efforts based on lessons learned over the years in North Karelia. Continuing experiences in this region can help in modifying future health education efforts in Russia.

Assistance from U.S. government agencies has helped to impart other local lessons for Russian health care (Wines, 2000d). A USAID program subsidizing health care partnerships assisted LaCrosse, Wisconsin, in helping its "sister city" of Dubna, Russia, cut its mortality rate 20 percent below national levels, eliminate the need for one-third of its hospital beds, and reduce the abortion rate to two-thirds the national level. Support from the U.S. Department of Health and Human Services led to public health instruction on tobacco and alcohol as early as the primary grades in Dubna. Dubna officials have visited LaCrosse to learn and apply to their hometown lessons in home health care and in improving maternal and infant health care by renovating a hospital to allow mothers and their newborns to stay together in private rooms.

HEALTH CARE SYSTEM AND FINANCING

Russia might also benefit from health lessons learned in other former Soviet states or client nations (Garrett, 2000). Turkmenistan in the 1990s improved its health—cutting maternal mortality 10 percent, measles by a third, anthrax by 60 percent, and eliminating polio—through a program that reduced hospitalization and trained fewer, better qualified physicians. Ukrainian health officials, with help from American sponsors, developed initiatives that cut both hospitalizations and deaths by nearly a third. Czech medical officials have been able to curb drug-resistant forms of disease by relying on central microbiology laboratories and limiting physician prescriptions of antibiotics. Estonia developed a more solid scientific establishment by pruning its weakest branches and providing more funding for its strongest.

Improving the health care system can lead both to short-term gains in combating epidemics and to long-term gains in being more responsive to modern health needs. Because of the ability of diseases like tuberculosis and HIV/AIDS to cross international borders, the international community has a direct interest in helping Russia reestablish its ability to control communicable and infectious diseases. Other initiatives Russia can undertake to improve its long-term health include emphasizing quality over quantity in medical care. This may mean downsizing personnel and upgrading acute-care services while placing more emphasis on preventive health strategies.[1]

Following decades of neglect, much of the Russian health care system needs more money to strengthen primary health care and to establish greater equity among regional health services. After peaking at more than 6 percent of the gross national product in the 1960s,

---

[1] Unfortunately, many of the general health reforms Russia needs may exacerbate problems of health care for the elderly. As Twigg (2001) notes, "older Russians simply do not present the 'patient profile' appropriate" for a shift to preventive and outpatient care, given their lack of mobility as well as the illnesses and complex treatments they often face. Furthermore, as Twigg notes, home health services designed especially for the elderly are virtually nonexistent. Nevertheless, there are some general health innovations, still in their infancy, from which the elderly may yet benefit. Some have suggested converting rural hospitals, being closed in structural reform of health care, to nursing homes, although there is little evidence of progress here. General practitioners are also receiving more training in geriatrics.

funding for Soviet health services was subject to a "residual principle," in which all other government services, particularly defense, were funded before health services were (Field, 2000). The Russian government has not completely reversed this decline in public health spending. The most recent comparable statistics show Russian health expenditures to comprise less than 5 percent of GDP, or about one-third the percentage in the United States (World Health Organization, 1999). Comparisons of health care spending as a percentage of the GDP understate the differences between health care spending in Russia and the United States because of the huge differences in GDP between the two nations. Russian per capita health care expenditures in 1995 were $148, about 4 percent of the U.S. level (Wines and Zuger, 2000). In 1999, the largest public hospital in Moscow spent $4.1 million to treat 35,000 patients, while a hospital complex of similar size in Brooklyn spent $565 million to treat 38,000 patients. Per capita health expenditures in Russia also trail those of Brazil, Mexico, Panama, South Africa, Thailand, and Venezuela (World Health Organization, 2000a).

Judicious spending of additional health care funds can help the Russian health care system improve in both the short and long term. Many Russians see a need for the government to do more to strengthen health care. One in six (17 percent) identify the "crises in health and education" as among the most pressing problems the government should address (Russian Center for Public Opinion and Market Research, 2000). When properly trained and funded, Russian health care facilities can be among the finest in the world, as some acclaim the Kremlin Hospital to be after its improvements, funded by American public and private donors, in recent years (Garrett, 2000).[2] A nascent private health care system in Russia is also making uneven strides toward modern facilities (Wines, 2000c). Some completely private clinics offer top-tier medical service for the small proportion

---

[2] Western concern over the health of Boris Yeltsin and its implications for the stability of the Russian government apparently led to the renovation of the Kremlin Hospital, which had deteriorated in the late 1980s and early 1990s (Garrett, 2000). In 1996, Yeltsin needed quadruple bypass cardiac surgery. No facility in Russia at that time could provide the level of care that Yeltsin would receive in the West, but it would have been impolitic for Yeltsin to seek care outside Russia. In response, the U.S. government arranged a hasty renovation of the Kremlin Hospital, including improvements to staff training and physical plant.

of the population able to pay for such quality. Other formerly public facilities mix public and private financing in catering to patients of all incomes, with the poorest patients subsidized by the government and paying clients (Wines, 2000c).

An antiquated hospital system with one-tenth of its hospitals built before World War I and one-fifth of its hospitals lacking running water (Wines and Zuger, 2000) cannot hope for all its facilities to soon reach 21st century standards. Yet simpler improvements, such as donations of surplus medical supplies from other nations, can help improve care. Russia has often lacked even the funds to accept equipment donations to alleviate its conditions. Swedish plans to donate surplus medical equipment from its military stalled, for example, because of Russian inability to pay for the transport of the equipment (O'Flynn, 2000).

Any changes in health care should take into greater account the regional differences Russia has in health care needs. As the Soviets cut health care spending they also shifted the costs of the system to the regions, but the regions face uneven health care needs. The increases in "civilization" diseases that have led to mortality increases among working-age populations are concentrated in the more densely populated western areas of the Russian Federation, where health care networks may be easier to repair and maintain. The sparsely populated eastern expanses of Russia face more elementary health care challenges, as indicated by infant mortality levels above those for the rest of the nation (Figure 6.1).

OTHER GOVERNMENT INITIATIVES

Not all initiatives that can be undertaken in the short term may prove successful. The antialcohol campaign of the 1980s appears to have helped cut Russian mortality, but its deep unpopularity led to its abandonment after just a few years. Russian officials have long had mixed attitudes on alcohol and its regulation, dating back to Imperial Russia (Shkolnikov and Nemtsov, 1997). Initially, the Bolsheviks saw alcohol as incompatible with a socialist society and therefore prohibited its sale. In 1927, however, the Stalin government permitted the state sale of alcoholic drinks to raise revenue for the development of socialist industry. Government officials rationalized later sales by

RANDMR1273-6.1

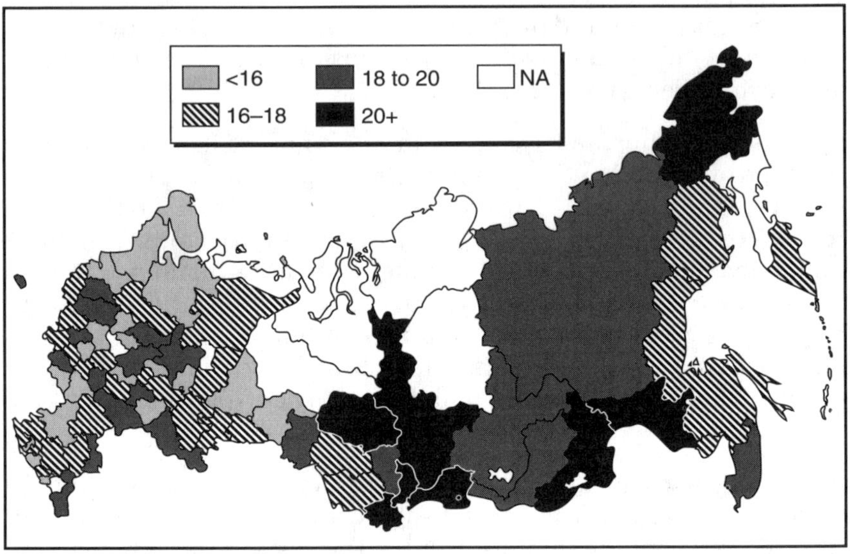

SOURCE: Pashintseva et al. (1998).

Figure 6.1—Infant Mortality Rate (Infant Deaths per 1,000 Live Births) by Region, 1997

insisting that heavy drinking and alcohol abuse were products of capitalist, and not socialist, societies, and that therefore alcohol abuse could not become a problem in the Soviet Union (Treml, 1997). Soviet officials continually had dual attitudes toward alcohol, on the one hand deploring the economic, health, and social problems it caused while, on the other, seeing it as a vital source of revenues for state needs. In the early 1990s, after the dissolution of the Soviet Union, sales of alcohol in Russia were deregulated, but there have been some modest, if contested, recent efforts to raise taxes on alcohol (Pronina, 2000). Russia may be better able to resolve its problems with alcohol consumption when it resolves official attitudes toward it.

Russia may improve its health care by reforming other parts of its government and society. In early 2001, the Duma approved legislation designed to reduce the number of prisoners in Russia by

250,000, or by about a fourth of the prison population of nearly one million, within the next two years (Uzelac, 2001). Such moves to ease overcrowding in the prisons, particularly if decreasing the number of nonviolent offenders awaiting trial in pretrial detention centers where tuberculosis is rampant,[3] could benefit society at large by reducing the number of persons exposed to the disease and liable to transmit it to others.

To better design both short- and long-term measures for its demographic stability, Russia must develop and use the technical expertise needed to collect and analyze regular statistics on its demographic conditions. Russia has a difficult Soviet legacy to overcome here. The Soviet government often suppressed or misinterpreted demographic data for political purposes. While the Soviets had many means to compel both participation and information gathering in past censuses, the Russian Goskomstat has had to create a new structure able to conduct a census of an emerging market society. The first post-Soviet census is scheduled for 2002. Assistance such as that the U.S. Census Bureau provides to other nations in developing statistical data might facilitate the Russian census.

LONG-TERM ISSUES

For its long-term demographic stability, Russia may have little choice but to rely on economic improvement. Russia may be able to curb the number of deaths now occurring annually, particularly among working-age males, but death is, after all, inevitable, especially in an aging society. This means that, absent higher birth rates, Russia may have to adjust to a smaller population. This may mean adjusting its national and international ambitions to those that a smaller population can justify, or adjusting its priorities to focus on domestic issues such as health and education rather than attempting to procure or maintain the trappings of a major world power. Russia has tried pronatalist policies to increase its population, but with little long-

[3] An earlier bill passed by the Duma to relieve prison overcrowding was scuttled when the Prosecutor General objected to provisions that shortened from 18 to 12 months the time a prisoner could be held in pretrial detention (Uzelac, 2001). The legislative compromise passed in February 2001 shortens the maximum pretrial detention time to 12 months while allowing those suspected of committing "grave" crimes to be detained for up to 18 months.

term effect. No nation yet has been able to sustain long the costs of pronatalist incentives.

Immigration can, theoretically, help stabilize a declining population, but this is not likely to be enough to stabilize the size of the Russian population. Immigration of ethnic Russians in recent years has been substantial, occasionally numbering more than a half million persons per year, but this has not been enough to offset the natural population losses that Russia has suffered. The number of ethnic Russians migrating to Russia from neighboring nations has declined in recent years, and it may be that most ethnic Russians desiring to move to Russia after the collapse of the Soviet Union have already done so. Russia would need an enormous number of immigrants to achieve population stability in future years. To maintain a constant total population in the next 50 years, for example, Russia would need to admit more than a half million immigrants annually, or more than it has admitted in nearly every year of its history (United Nations Population Division, 2000). Such a scenario would mean that, by 2050, about one-fourth of the Russian population would comprise migrants of the first half of the 21st century or their descendants. Given reports (Feifer, 2000; Mereu, 2000; Kagarlitsky, 2000) of official and popular xenophobia in many locations, including Moscow, it is unclear that Russia can tolerate such massive infusions of foreign populations. Russians also may perceive a security threat posed by migration in certain areas. In the sparsely populated Russian Far East, many Russians fear a security threat from Chinese migration, spurred in part by Chinese historical claims to much territory that is now in Russia (Working, 2000). Large differences in population density along the border add to Russian security concerns, with the population density on the Chinese side being 15 to 30 times that of the Russian side (Zayonchkovskaya, 1999b). Finally, as the American experience shows, immigration is not always a panacea.

The deepest demographic problems might be solved only by long-term economic stability and resulting improvements in the economy and public finance. Economic improvements may help improve Russian health directly and indirectly by inducing behaviors that are both healthier and more productive for the economy, in turn yielding demographic benefits such as population stability. Several formerly communist states of Eastern Europe brought their mortality under control once they reached macroeconomic stability (Brainerd, 1998).

In these cases, government policy has not been as important as stable and sustained economic growth in affecting mortality.

Russian mortality stopped rising when the economy stabilized in the mid-1990s, but deaths increased following the economic crisis in 1998. The Russian economy has grown in three of the past four years, but it still has a very long way to go to recover what it has lost in the past decade, when real gross domestic product per capita declined by about 40 percent. There are questions of how well Russia can maintain its recent economic momentum, especially should the boosts provided to the Russian economy by higher prices for Russian petroleum or ruble devaluation wear off, or should inflation spike in response to the printing of rubles to purchase foreign currency used to buy Russian exports (Kovalyova, 2000; Latsis, 2000).

Nevertheless, recent economic changes—including the role of ruble devaluation in making Russian products competitive with imports, thus reviving domestic manufactures and consequent tax revenues—have helped give Russia a window of economic opportunity in which the government can improve its long-term financial health and turn its attention to structural changes (Sokolowski, 2000). Despite some missteps, International Monetary Fund programs have also helped Russia to live within its means, thus stabilizing both the economy and the public budget. In addition to its economic window of opportunity, Russia has, as we saw earlier, a demographic window of opportunity to prepare for growing pension obligations in future years.

In the wake of recent improvements, however modest, more Russians are offering at least guarded optimism about the future (Russian Center for Public Opinion and Market Research, 2000). Whereas in July 1999 nearly half (48 percent) of Russians said the situation in the country was "unbearable," by March 2001 two in three were saying the situation was "difficult but bearable" (50 percent) or that "things are not so bad" (15 percent). Still, the question remains open of when Russia will attain stable economic growth of sufficient magnitude to help solve its health problems.

To some, the question may remain open of whether Russia is experiencing a true demographic "crisis" or whether it is seeing a particularly striking and unfortunate confluence of social and economic trends resulting from a slow transition and demographic trends, such as declining fertility, that are occurring elsewhere as well. Regardless of whether Russia is suffering a demographic "crisis" or the culmination of decades-long demographic trends, it is clear that population growth alone will not suffice now to improve the political and economic situation. As a Russian family planning official noted, "A simple rise in the birth rate is not enough. Russia needs more people, but it needs more intelligent, healthy people, not more beggars and alcoholics" (Uzelac, 2000b). Until the Russian economy and society are able to provide for the Russian people not just to increase quantitatively but also to flourish qualitatively, the dire demographic problems Russia faces, and the limited Russian ability to deal with them, may persist.

BIBLIOGRAPHY

Agence France Presse, "Russia Carried Out 2.5 Million Abortions in 1997," November 29, 1998.

Agence France Presse, "Infant Mortality Rate in Russia Drops: Health Officials," March 21, 2001a.

Agence France Presse, "Tuberculosis Rate in Russia Jumps Five Percent in 2000," March 21, 2001b.

Anderson, Barbara A., and Brian D. Silver, "Issues of Data Quality in Assessing Mortality Trends and Levels in the New Independent States," in José Luis Bobadilla, Christine A. Costello, and Faith Mitchell, eds., *Premature Death in the New Independent States*, Washington, D.C.: National Academy Press, 1997, pp. 120–155.

Andreev, Evgeni, Sergei Scherbov, and Frans Willekens, "Population of Russia: What Can We Expect in the Future?" *World Development*, Vol. 26, No. 11, 1998, pp. 1939–1955.

Andreev, Evgueni, "The Dynamics of Mortality in the Russian Federation," in United Nations and Flemish Scientific Institute, *Health and Mortality Issues of Global Concern*, 1999, pp. 262–290.

Avdeev, Alexandr, "Contraception and Abortions: Trends and Prospects for the 1990s," in Wolfgang Lutz, Sergei Scherbov, and Andrei Volkov, eds., *Demographic Trends and Patterns in the Soviet Union Before 1991*, London: Routledge, 1994, pp. 131–146.

Avdeev, Alexandre, and Irina Troitskaia, "New Features in Abortion Dynamics in Russia in the 1990s," paper presented to the European Population Conference held at The Hague, 1999.

Badkhen, Anna, "Journalists Not Immune to Prejudice," *Moscow Times*, September 12, 2000.

Ball, Deborah Yarsike, "The Social Crisis of the Russian Military," in Mark G. Field and Judyth L. Twigg, eds., *Russia's Torn Safety Nets: Health and Social Welfare During the Transition*, New York: St. Martin's Press, 2000, pp. 271–287.

Bazhenova, Anna, "Millions Infertile in Russia, Say Doctors," ITAR-TASS, March 16, 2001a.

Bazhenova, Anna, "Russia to Have Over 1 Million HIV-Infected by Year End," ITAR-TASS, April 3, 2001b.

Bloom, David E., and Pia N. Malaney, 1998, "Macroeconomic Consequences of the Russian Mortality Crisis," *World Development*, Vol. 26, No. 11, November 1998, pp. 2073–2085.

Bohlen, Celestine, "Russian Women Turning to Abortion Less Often," *New York Times*, March 29, 1999.

Bongaarts, John, and Rodolfo A. Bulatao, eds., *Beyond Six Billion: Forecasting the World's Population*, Washington, D.C.: National Academy Press, 2000.

Brainerd, Elizabeth, "Market Reform and Mortality in Transition Economies," *World Development*, Vol. 26, No. 11, November 1998, pp. 2013–2027.

Brown, Virginia, "Pills and Tests for Relationships of the '90s," *Moscow Times*, January 29, 1997.

Buckley, Cynthia, electronic mail to Clifford Grammich, October 31, 2000.

Buckley, Cynthia, "Family Matters: Intergenerational Wealth Transfers and Survival Networks," paper presented at University of Texas-Austin conference "From Red to Gray: Aging in the Russian Federation," April 2001.

Buckley, Cynthia, and Dennis Donahue, "Promises to Keep: Pension Provision in the Russian Federation," in Mark G. Field and Judyth L. Twigg, eds., *Russia's Torn Safety Nets: Health and Social Welfare During the Transition*, New York: St. Martin's Press, 2000, pp. 251–270.

Bulatao, Rodolfo A., *The Value of Family Planning Programs in Developing Countries*, Santa Monica, Calif.: RAND, MR-978, 1998. See http://www.rand.org/publications/MR/MR978/ (as of April 16, 2001).

Burke, Justin, "Internal Migration: A Civil Society Challenge," in Mark G. Field and Judyth L. Twigg, eds., *Russia's Torn Safety Nets: Health and Social Welfare During the Transition*, New York: St. Martin's Press, 2000, pp. 213–230.

Chandler, Andrea, "Political and Institutional Dimensions of Russia's Old-Age Pension Crisis," paper presented at University of Texas-Austin conference "From Red to Gray: Aging in the Russian Federation," April 2001.

Chen, Lincoln C., Friederike Wittgenstein, and Elizabeth McKeon, "The Upsurge of Mortality in Russia: Causes and Policy Implications," *Population and Development Review*, Vol. 22, No. 3, September 1996, pp. 517–530.

Chenet, Laurent, Martin McKee, David Leon, Vladimir Shkolnikov, and Sergei Vassin, "Alcohol and Cardiovascular Mortality in Moscow," *Journal of Epidemiology and Community Health*, Vol. 52, No. 12, December 1998, pp. 772–774.

DaVanzo, Julie, ed., *Russia's Demographic "Crisis,"* Santa Monica, Calif.: RAND, CF-124, 1996. See http://www.rand.org/publications/CF/CF124/ (as of April 16, 2001).

DaVanzo, Julie, and David Adamson, *Russia's Demographic "Crisis": How Real Is It?*, Santa Monica, Calif.: RAND, IP-162, July 1997. See http://www.rand.org/publications/IP/IP162/ (as of April 16, 2001).

DaVanzo, Julie, and Clifford Grammich, "Barren Ground: Eastern Europe's Transition from Communism Isn't the Only Factor Affecting the Region's Demographics," *Transitions Online*, June

12, 2000. Also available at http://www.rand.org/popmatters/TOL.html (as of April 16, 2001).

David, Henry P., "Overview," in Henry P. David, ed., *From Abortion to Contraception: A Resource to Public Policies and Reproductive Behavior in Central and Eastern Europe from 1917 to the Present,* Westport, Conn.: Greenwood Press, 1999, pp. 3–22.

Dolgov, Anna, "Over Half of Russian Newborns Experience Postnatal Problems," *Moscow Times,* October 7, 2000.

Eberstadt, Nicholas, "Health and Mortality in Eastern Europe, 1965–85," *Communist Economies,* Vol. 2, No. 3, 1990, pp. 347–371.

Eberstadt, Nicholas, "Russia: Too Sick to Matter?" *Policy Review,* No. 95, June 1999. See http://www.policyreview.com/jun99/eberstadt.html (as of April 16, 2001).

Entwistle, Barbara, and Polina Kozyreva, "New Estimates of Induced Abortion in Russia," *Studies in Family Planning,* Vol. 28, No. 1, March 1997, pp. 14–23.

Farmer, Paul E., et al., *The Global Impact of Drug-Resistant Tuberculosis,* Cambridge, Mass.: Harvard Medical School and Open Society Institute, 1999. See http://www.soros.org/tb/index.html (as of April 16, 2001).

Fedorov, Yuri, ed., *Human Development Report 1999, Russian Federation,* Moscow: United Nations Development Programme and Human Rights Publishers, 1999.

Feifer, Gregory, "Moscow Sets Foreign-Worker Quotas," *Moscow Times,* March 10, 2000.

Felgenhauer, Pavel, "Defense Dossier: A Reform That Doesn't Hurt," *Moscow Times,* November 16, 2000a.

Felgenhauer, Pavel, "Defense Dossier: Is Putin Playing the Liberal?" *Moscow Times,* November 23, 2000b.

Feshbach, Murray, *Ecological Disaster: Cleaning Up the Hidden Legacy of the Soviet Regime,* New York: Twentieth Century Fund, 1995.

Feshbach, Murray, "An AIDS Catastrophe," *Moscow Times,* January 14, 2000.

Feshbach, Murray, "Russia's Population Meltdown," *The Wilson Quarterly,* Vol. 25, No. 1, Winter 2001.

Field, Mark G., "The Health and Demographic Crisis in Post-Soviet Russia," in Mark G. Field and Judyth L. Twigg, eds., *Russia's Torn Safety Nets: Health and Social Welfare During the Transition,* New York: St. Martin's Press, 2000, pp. 11–42.

Garrett, Laurie, *Betrayal of Trust: The Collapse of Global Public Health,* New York: Hyperion, 2000.

Gerber, Ted, "Opportunity or Desperation? The Elderly and the Labor Market in the Post-Soviet Era," paper presented at University of Texas-Austin conference "From Red to Gray: Aging in the Russian Federation," April 2001.

Goldberg, Daniel, electronic mail to Julie DaVanzo, December 7, 2000a.

Goldberg, Daniel, electronic mail to Clifford Grammich, December 19, 2000b.

Goldberg, Howard, Valentina Bodrova, Ani Shakarishvili, and Douglas Storey, *1996 Russia Women's Reproductive Health Survey: A Study of Three Sites, Final Report,* Washington, D.C.: U.S. Agency for International Development, 1998.

Gorbacheva, Ada, "Collapse of Public Health," *Nezaviimaya Gazeta,* March 21, 2001.

Grange, John M., and Alimuddin Zumla, "Paradox of the Global Emergency of Tuberculosis," *The Lancet,* Vol. 353, March 20, 1999, p. 996.

Harrigan, Steve, report from Moscow, "CNN Today," Cable News Network, November 23, 2000.

Heleniak, Timothy, "Russia's Demographic Dilemma," *CERES Newsletter,* Washington, D.C.: Georgetown University, February 2001a.

Heleniak, Timothy, "Geographic Aspects of Population Aging in the Russian Federation," paper presented at University of Texas-Austin conference "From Red to Gray: Aging in the Russian Federation," April 2001b.

Hoyert, Donna L., Kenneth D. Kochanek, and Sherry L. Murphy, "Deaths: Final Data for 1997," *National Vital Statistics Reports*, Vol. 47, No. 19, June 30, 1999. See http://www.cdc.gov/nchs/data/nvs47_19.pdf (as of April 16, 2001).

Institut National d'Études Démographiques, *Démographie de la Russie et de son Empire sur la Toile*, 2000. Available at http://www-census.ined.fr/demogrus/ (as of April 16, 2001).

Interfax, "Number of HIV and AIDS Patients Increases Four Times in Russia," March 11, 2001.

Kagarlitsky, Boris, "Racial Purity Never Goes Out of Style," *Moscow Times*, December 2, 2000.

Karush, Sarah, "'99 Census Postponed Indefinitely," *Moscow Times*, July 3, 1999.

Karush, Sarah, "Schools Fret over Teacher Deficit," *Moscow Times*, August 26, 2000.

Karush, Sarah, "Cabinet Tackles Population Crisis," *Moscow Times*, February 16, 2001.

Kingkade, Ward, "Population Trends: Russia," U.S. Census Bureau International Brief IB/96-2, February 1997. Available at http://www.census.gov/ipc/prod/ib96-2.pdf (as of April 16, 2001).

Klomegah, Kester, "When One Wife Is Not Enough," *Moscow Times*, February 2, 2001.

Klyshnikov, Vladimir, "Reproductive Resources of Russia," *Meditsinskaya Gazeta*, December 29, 1999.

Kovalyova, Svetlana, "Kudrin Warns of Slower Growth," *Moscow Times*, September 13, 2000.

Krindatch, Alexei D., 1996, *Geography of Religions in Russia*, Decatur, Georgia: Glenmary Research Center.

Krupenik, Nikolai, "UN Says There Are 300,000 HIV-infected People in Russia," ITAR-TASS, March 10, 2001.

Lagnado, Alice, "Exodus as Thousands Flee from Russian Anti-Semites," *Telegraph*, June 6, 1999. See http://www.telegraph.co.uk:80/et?ac=004553952760174&rtmo=LxxLxbid&atmo=rrrrrrrq&pg=/et/99/6/6/wrus06.html (as of April 16, 2001).

Latsis, Otto, "Russian Economy Heating Up," *The Russia Journal*, July 13, 2000.

Leon, David A., and Vladimir M. Shkolnikov, "Social Stress and the Russian Mortality Crisis," *Journal of the American Medical Association*, Vol. 279, March 11, 1998, pp. 790–791.

Lorimer, Frank, *The Population of the Soviet Union: History and Prospects*, Geneva: League of Nations, 1946.

MacWilliam, Ian, "Russia on Verge of AIDS Epidemic, Expert Says," *Moscow Times*, May 15, 1997.

McCarthy, Kevin, *World Population Shifts: Boom or Doom?* Santa Monica, California: RAND, DB-308, 2001.

Medvedev, Zhores, "Russia's Alcoholic Myth," *Moscow Times*, June 28, 1996.

Mereu, Francesca, "Foreigners Get Rough Deal at Hands of Moscow Press," *The Russia Journal*, July 10, 2000.

Meslé, France, Vladimir M. Shkolnikov, Véronique Hertrich, and Jacques Vallin, *Tendances récentes de la mortalité par cause en Russie 1965–1994* and electronic data diskettes, Moscow: Centre de Démographie et d'Écologie Humaine, 1996.

Minakir, Pavel A., "Chinese Immigration in the Russian Far East: Regional, National, and International Dimensions," in Jeremy R. Azrael and Emil A. Payin, eds., *Cooperation and Conflict in the Former Soviet Union: Implications for Migration*, Santa Monica, Calif.: RAND CF-130, 1996, pp. 85–97. See http://www.rand.org/publications/CF/CF130/CF130ch7.pdf (as of April 16, 2001).

Mroz, Thomas, Dominic Mancini, and Barry Popkin, "Monitoring Economic Conditions in the Russian Federation: The Russia

Longitudinal Monitoring Survey 1992–98," report submitted to the U.S. Agency for International Development, Carolina Population Center, University of North Carolina at Chapel Hill, March 1999. See http://www.cpc.unc.edu/projects/rlms/papers/Econ1998.pdf (as of April 16, 2001).

National Center for Health Statistics, *Health, United States, 1999, with Health and Aging Chartbook*, Hyattsville, Md., 1999. See http://www.cdc.gov/nchs/data/hus99.pdf (as of April 16, 2001).

Naumova, T. V., "Russia's 'Brain Drain'," trans. Kim Braithwaite, *Russian Social Science Review*, Vol. 39, No. 2, July 1998, pp. 49–56.

Netto, Eduardo M., Christopher Dye, Sonja Schmidt, and Mario Ravglione, *Global Tuberculosis Control, WHO Report on the Global Tuberculosis Epidemic 1998*, Geneva: World Health Organization. See http://www.who.int/gtb/publications/tbrep_98/PDF/tbrep98.pdf (as of December 22, 2000).

New York Times, "Russians Vanishing," December 6, 2000.

Nichiporuk, Brian, *The Security Dynamics of Demographic Factors*, Santa Monica, Calif.: RAND, MR-1088, 2000. See http://www.rand.org/publications/MR/MR1088/ (as of April 16, 2001).

Notzon, Francis C., Yuri M. Komarov, Sergei P. Ermakov, Christopher T. Sempos, James S. Marks, and Elena V. Sempos, "Causes of Declining Life Expectancy in Russia," *Journal of the American Medical Association*, Vol. 279, March 11, 1998, pp. 793–800.

O'Flynn, Kevin, "Aid to Prisons, Hospitals Left Stranded in Sweden," *Moscow Times*, October 13, 2000.

Pashintseva, N. I., I. V. Voronina, and L. A. Kazachenko, *The Demographic Yearbook of Russia, Statistical Handbook*, Moscow: State Committee of the Russian Federation on Statistics (RF Goskomstat), 1998.

Perevedentsev, Victor, "The Demographic Situation in Post-Soviet Russia," in George J. Demko, Grigory Ioffe, and Zhanna Zayonchkovskaya, eds., *Population Under Duress: The Geodemography of Post-Soviet Russia*, Boulder, Colo.: Westview Press, 1999, pp. 17–40.

Peterson, Demosthenes J., "The Number and Cost of Illegal Abortions in the USSR," Berkeley-Duke Occasional Papers on the Second Economy in the USSR, No. 9, February 1987.

Peterson, D. J., *Troubled Lands: The Legacy of Soviet Environmental Destruction*, Boulder, Colo.: Westview Press, 1993. See http://www.rand.org/centers/cre/troubledlands/ (as of April 16, 2001).

Pierce, John P., "Tobacco Control Policy Strategies: Lessons from Western Developed Countries," in José Luis Bobadilla, Christine A. Costello, and Faith Mitchell, eds., *Premature Death in the New Independent States*, Washington, D.C.: National Academy Press, 1997, pp. 287–313.

Piper, Elizabeth, "AIDS Threatens Russians More than Chechen Fighting," Reuters, December 1, 1999.

Popkin, Barry, Namvar Zohoori, Lenore Kohlmeier, Alexander Baturin, Arseni Martinchik, and Alexander Deev, "Nutritional Risk Factors in the Former Soviet Union," in José Luis Bobadilla, Christine A. Costello, and Faith Mitchell, eds., *Premature Death in the New Independent States*, Washington: National Academy Press, 1997, pp. 314–334.

Popov, Andrej A., "Family Planning and Induced Abortion in Post-Soviet Russia of the Early 1990s: Unmet Needs in Information Supply," in Julie DaVanzo, ed., *Russia's Demographic "Crisis,"* Santa Monica, Calif.: RAND CF-124, 1996, pp. 84–111. See http://www.rand.org/publications/CF/CF124/CF124.chap3.html (as of April 16, 2001).

Popov, Andrej A., and Henry P. David, "Russian Federation and USSR Successor States," in Henry P. David, ed., *From Abortion to Contraception: A Resource to Public Policies and Reproductive Behavior in Central and Eastern Europe from 1917 to the Present*, Westport, Conn.: Greenwood Press, 1999, pp. 223–277.

Popov, Vladimir, "Demographic Trends and Economic Performance During Transition: The Russian Experience," paper presented at University of Texas-Austin conference "From Red to Gray: Aging in the Russian Federation," April 2001.

Powell, David E., "The Problem of AIDS," in Mark G. Field and Judyth L. Twigg, eds., *Russia's Torn Safety Nets: Health and Social Welfare During the Transition*, New York: St. Martin's Press, 2000, pp. 123–151.

Prokhorov, Alexander V., "Cigarette Smoking and Priorities for Tobacco Control in the New Independent States," in José Luis Bobadilla, Christine A. Costello, and Faith Mitchell, eds., *Premature Death in the New Independent States*, Washington, D.C.: National Academy Press, 1997, pp. 275–286.

Pronina, Lyuba, "Duma Attacks Alcohol Tax Hike," *Moscow Times*, June 22, 2000.

Puska, Pekka, "Chronic Disease Prevention in the New Independent States: Finnish Experiences," José Luis Bobadilla, Christine A. Costello, and Faith Mitchell, eds., *Premature Death in the New Independent States*, Washington, D.C.: National Academy Press, 1997, pp. 335–354.

Rahman, Mizanur, Julie DaVanzo, and Abdur Razzaque, "Do Better Family Planning Services Reduce Abortion? Evidence from Matlab, Bangladesh," *The Lancet*, forthcoming.

Ravglione, Mario, Paul P. Nunn, Arata Kochi, and Richard J. O'Brien, "The Pandemic of HIV-Associated Tuberculosis," in Jonathan M. Mann and Daniel J. M. Tarantola, eds., *AIDS in the World II: Global Dimensions, Social Roots, and Responses*, New York: Oxford University Press, 1996, pp. 87–96.

Reuters, "Putin Signs Russia's New Military Doctrine," April 23, 2000a.

Reuters, "Putin Sees Strong, Free Russia, Liberal Economy," July 9, 2000b.

Rozenfeld, Boris A., "The Crisis of Russian Health Care and Attempts at Reform," in Julie DaVanzo, ed., *Russia's Demographic "Crisis,"* Santa Monica, Calif.: RAND CF-124, 1996, pp. 163–173. See http://www.rand.org/publications/CF/CF124/CF124.chap5.html (as of April 16, 2001).

Russian Center for Public Opinion and Market Research (VCIOM) and University of Strathclyde Centre for the Study of Public Policy, *Russia Votes*, 2000. Available at http://www.russiavotes.org (as of December 22, 2000).

Russian Federation Ministry of Health, *Naselenie Rossii 1998 Annual Demographic Report*, Moscow: Centre for Demographic and Human Ecology, 1999.

Russian Federation State Committee on Statistics (RF Goskomstat), *Russia 1999*, 1999a. Available at http://www.gks.ru/scripts/eng/1c.exe?XXXX09R.1 (as of December 18, 2000).

Russian Federation State Committee on Statistics (RF Goskomstat), *Russia in Figures 1999*, 1999b. Available at http://www.gks.ru/scripts/eng/1c.exe?XXXX12R.1 (as of December 18, 2000).

Russian Federation State Committee on Statistics (RF Goskomstat), *Current Statistical Survey No. 31*, 1999c. Available at http://www.gks.ru/scripts/eng/1c.exe?XXXX06R.1 (as of December 22, 2000).

Shkolnikov, Vladimir D., "Potential Energy: Emergent Emigration of Highly Qualified Manpower from the Former Soviet Union," Dissertation, The RAND Graduate School, Santa Monica, Calif.: RAND, RGSD-13, 1995.

Shkolnikov, Vladimir M., electronic mail to Julie DaVanzo, April 22, 1997.

Shkolnikov, Vladimir M., electronic mail to Julie DaVanzo, February 19, 1998.

Shkolnikov, Vladimir M., Giovanni A. Cornia, David A. Leon, and France Meslé, "Causes of the Russian Mortality Crisis: Evidence and Interpretations," *World Development*, Vol. 26, No. 11, November 1998, pp. 1995–2011.

Shkolnikov, Vladimir M., and France Meslé, "The Russian Epidemiological Crisis as Mirrored by Mortality Trends," in Julie DaVanzo, ed., *Russia's Demographic "Crisis,"* Santa Monica, Calif.: RAND CF-124, 1996, pp. 113–161. See http://www.rand.org/publications/CF/CF124/CF124/cf124.chap4.html (as of June 29, 2001).

Shkolnikov, Vladimir M., France Meslé, and Jacques Vallin, "Recent Trends in Life Expectancy and Causes of Death in Russia," in José Luis Bobadilla, Christine A. Costello, and Faith Mitchell, eds., *Premature Death in the New Independent States,* Washington, D.C.: National Academy Press, 1997, pp. 34–65.

Shkolnikov, Vladimir M., and Alexander Nemtsov, "The Antialcohol Campaign and Variations in Russian Mortality," in José Luis Bobadilla, Christine A. Costello, and Faith Mitchell, eds., *Premature Death in the New Independent States,* Washington, D.C.: National Academy Press, 1997, pp. 239–261.

Sokolowski, Alexander, "Putin's Good Fortune," *Moscow Times,* December 22, 2000.

Specter, Michael, "Critical Condition—Russia's Degenerating Health: Rampant Illness, Shorter Lives," *New York Times,* February 19, 1995.

Stloukal, Libor, "Understanding the 'Abortion Culture' in Central and Eastern Europe," in Henry P. David, ed., *From Abortion to Contraception: A Resource to Public Policies and Reproductive Behavior in Central and Eastern Europe from 1917 to the Present,* Westport, Conn.: Greenwood Press, 1999, pp. 23–37.

Stone, Richard, "Stress: The Invisible Hand in Eastern Europe's Death Rates," *Science,* Vol. 288, June 9, 2000, pp. 1732–1733.

Taylor, Terence, ed., *The Military Balance 1999–2000,* London: Oxford University Press/International Institute for Strategic Studies, 1999.

Treml, Vladimir G., "Soviet and Russian Statistics on Alcohol Consumption and Abuse," in José Luis Bobadilla, Christine A. Costello, and Faith Mitchell, eds., *Premature Death in the New Independent States,* Washington, D.C.: National Academy Press, 1997, pp. 220–238.

Tsapenko, I. P., and A. V. Yurevich, "A Scientist in Business," *Herald of the Russian Academy of Sciences,* Vol. 69, No. 1, 1999, pp. 13–18.

Tuchinsky, Theodore H., and Elena A. Varavikova, 1996, "Addressing the Epidemiologic Transition in the Former Soviet Union:

Strategies for Health System and Public Health Reform in Russia," *American Journal of Public Health*, Vol. 86, No. 3, March 1996, pp. 313–320.

Twigg, Judyth L., "Unfulfilled Hopes: The Struggle to Reform Russian Health Care and Its Financing," in Mark G. Field and Judyth L. Twigg, eds., *Russia's Torn Safety Nets: Health and Social Welfare During the Transition*, New York: St. Martin's Press, 2000, pp. 43–64.

Twigg, Judyth L., "Health Care for the Elderly in Today's Russia: How Is It Delivered, and Who Pays?" paper presented at University of Texas-Austin conference "From Red to Gray: Aging in the Russian Federation," April 2001.

UNAIDS (Joint United Nations Programme on HIV/AIDS), *Report on the Global HIV/AIDS Epidemic*, Geneva, June 2000. See http://www.unaids.org/epidemic%5Fupdate/report/Epi_report.pdf (as of December 21, 2000).

United Nations Economic Commission for Europe, "Fertility Decline in the Transition Economies, 1989–1998: Economic and Social Factors Revisited," *The Economic Survey of Europe, 2000 No. 1*, Geneva, 2000, pp. 189–208. See http://www.unece.org/ead/pub/001/001_6.pdf (as of April 16, 2001).

United Nations Population Division, *Replacement Migration*, New York, 2000.

United Press International, "Russian City Declares AIDS Epidemic," June 7, 2000.

United States Agency for International Development, *1999 Russia Women's Reproductive Health Survey: Follow-up Study of Three Sites, Preliminary Report*, March 2000.

United States Bureau of Labor Statistics, "Employment status of the civilian noninstitutional population, 1936 to date," 2000. Available at http://www.bls.gov/pdf/cpsa1999.pdf (as of April 16, 2001).

United States Census Bureau, *Statistical Abstract of the United States 1999*, 1999. See http://www.census.gov/prod/www/statistical-abstract-us.html (as of December 20, 2000).

United States Census Bureau, *International Data Base*, 2000. Available at http://www.census.gov/ipc/www/idbnew.html (as of April 16, 2001).

Uzelac, Ana, "World Engaged in TB Fight," *Moscow Times*, March 25, 2000a.

Uzelac, Ana, "Demographics Show Fall in Population," *Moscow Times*, July 12, 2000b.

Uzelac, Ana, "Prisons Bill Sent to Upper House Again," *Moscow Times*, February 22, 2001.

Vassin, Sergei A., "The Determinants and Implications of an Aging Population in Russia," in Julie DaVanzo, ed., *Russia's Demographic "Crisis,"* Santa Monica, Calif.: RAND CF-124, 1996, pp. 175–200.

Vedomosti, Olga Romanova, "No. 1 Number Cruncher Readies for '02 Count," *Moscow Times*, February 28, 2001.

Velkoff, Victoria A., and Kevin Kinsella, "Russia's Aging Population," in Mark G. Field and Judyth L. Twigg, eds., *Russia's Torn Safety Nets: Health and Social Welfare During the Transition*, New York: St. Martin's Press, 2000, pp. 231–250.

Vishnevskii, A., "The Demographic Potential of Russia," trans. Robert Valliere, *Russian Social Science Review*, Vol. 40, No. 4, July 1999, pp. 4–29.

Vishnevsky, Anatoly G., "Family, Fertility, and Demographic Dynamics in Russia: Analysis and Forecast," in Julie DaVanzo, ed., *Russia's Demographic "Crisis,"* Santa Monica, Calif.: RAND CF-124, 1996, pp. 1–34. See http://www.rand.org/publications/CF/CF124/CF124.chap1.html (as of April 16, 2001).

Vitkovskaya, Galina, "Potential Migration of Russian-Speaking Populations from Central Asia to Russia," in George J. Demko, Grigory Ioffe, and Zhanna Zayonchkovskaya, eds., *Population Under Duress: The Geodemography of Post-Soviet Russia*, Boulder, Colo.: Westview Press, 1999, pp. 149–176.

Walberg, Peder, Martin McKee, Vladimir M. Shkolnikov, Laurent Chenet, and David A. Leon, "Economic Change, Crime, and

Mortality Crisis in Russia: Regional Analysis," *British Medical Journal*, Vol. 317, August 1, 1998, pp. 312–318.

Williams, Carol J., "A Role Reversal in Russia," *Los Angeles Times*, August 15, 1996.

Wines, Michael, "The Siberian Side of AIDS," *Moscow Times*, April 29, 2000a.

Wines, Michael, "Freedom's Toll—An Ailing Russia Lives a Tough Life That's Getting Shorter," *New York Times*, December 3, 2000b.

Wines, Michael, "Capitalism Comes to Russian Health Care," *New York Times*, December 22, 2000c.

Wines, Michael, "Freedom's Toll—A Fit City Offers Russia a Self-Help Model," *New York Times*, December 31, 2000d.

Wines, Michael, and Abigail Zuger, "Freedom's Toll—In Russia, the Ill and Infirm Include Health Care Itself," *New York Times*, December 4, 2000.

Wolfe, Elizabeth, "Medical Center Has a Family Focus," *Moscow Times*, June 27, 2000.

Working, Russell, "Will Chinese Roots Grow?" *Moscow Times*, July 4, 2000.

World Health Organization, *World Health Statistics Annual*, Geneva, 1998.

World Health Organization, *The World Health Report 1999: Making a Difference*, Geneva, 1999. See http://www.who.int/whr/1999/en/pdf/whr99.pdf (as of April 16, 2001).

World Health Organization, *Full Report: The World Health Report 2000*, Geneva, 2000a. See http://www.who.int/whr/2000/en/report.htm (as of April 16, 2001).

World Health Organization, "WHO Estimates of Health Personnel," 2000b. Available at http://www-nt.who.int/whosis/statistics/health_personnel/health_personnel.cfm?path=statistics,health_personnel&language=english (as of April 16, 2001).

World Health Organization, Regional Office for Europe, *Health for All Data Base—European Region*, June 2000c, Copenhagen. Available at http://www.who.dk.

Wulf, Deirdre, *Sharing Responsibility: Women, Society, and Abortion Worldwide*, New York: The Alan Guttmacher Institute, 1999.

Yablokova, Oksana, "Population Takes Biggest Plunge Yet," *Moscow Times*, January 26, 2000a.

Yablokova, Oksana, "Delayed 2002 Census Gets Trial Run," *Moscow Times*, October 12, 2000b.

Yurevich, A. V., and I. P. Tsapenko, "Intellectual Emigration from Russia," *Herald of the Russian Academy of Sciences*, Vol. 68, No. 4, 1998, pp. 346–350.

Zakharov, Sergei, "Fertility, Nuptiality, and Family Planning in Russia: Problems and Prospects," in George J. Demko, Grigory Ioffe, and Zhanna Zayonchkovskaya, eds., *Population Under Duress: The Geodemography of Post-Soviet Russia*, Boulder, Colo.: Westview Press, 1999a, pp. 41–58.

Zakharov, Sergei V., "Fertility Trends in Russia and the European Newly Independent States: Crisis or Turning Point?" *Population Bulletin of the United Nations*, Nos. 40/41, 1999b, pp. 292–317.

Zakharov, Sergei V., "Unlike Their Parents, the Russian Youth Are Less Eager to Form Families at Young Ages: Basic Outcomes from the Analyses of Period and Cohort Parity-Specific Fertility Tables, 1979–1987," paper presented to Second Workshop on Lowest Low Fertility, Max Planck Institute for Demographic Research, Rostock, Germany, December 1999c.

Zakharov, Sergei V., letter to Robert Schoeni, October 26, 2000a.

Zakharov, Sergei V., electonic mail to Julie DaVanzo, December 19, 2000b.

Zakharov, Sergei V., and Elena I. Ivanova, "Fertility Decline and Recent Changes in Russia: On the Threshold of the Second Demographic Transition," in Julie DaVanzo, ed., *Russia's Demographic "Crisis,"* Santa Monica, Calif.: RAND CF-124, 1996, pp. 36–82. See http://www.rand.org/publications/CF/CF124/CF124.chap2.html (as of April 16, 2001).

Zaslavskaia, Tatjana I., and Valentina A. Kalmyk, *Sotsial'no-ekonomicheskoe razvitie sela i migratsiia naseleniia,* Novoskbirsk, Russia: Institut ekon. i organ. promyshl. proizfod., 1972.

Zaionchkovskaya, Zhanna A., "Migration Patterns in the Former Soviet Union," in Jeremy R. Azrael and Emil A. Payin, eds., *Cooperation and Conflict in the Former Soviet Union: Implications for Migration,* Santa Monica, Calif.: RAND CF-130, 1996, pp. 15–48. See http://www.rand.org/publications/CF/CF130/CF130ch2.pdf (as of April 16, 2001).

Zayonchkovskaya, Zhanna, "Recent Migration Trends in Russia," in George J. Demko, Grigory Ioffe, and Zhanna Zayonchkovskaya, eds., *Population Under Duress: The Geodemography of Post-Soviet Russia,* Boulder, Colo.: Westview Press, 1999a, pp. 107–136.

Zayonchkovskaya, Zhanna, "Chinese Demographic Expansion into Russia: Myth or Inevitability?" in George J. Demko, Grigory Ioffe, and Zhanna Zayonchkovskaya, eds., *Population Under Duress: The Geodemography of Post-Soviet Russia,* Boulder, Colo.: Westview Press, 1999b, pp.137–148.

Zohoori, Namvar, Laura Henderson, Karin Gleiter, and Barry Popkin, "Monitoring Health Conditions in the Russian Federation: The Russian Longitudinal Monitoring Survey 1992–98," report submitted to the U.S. Agency for International Development, Carolina Population Center, University of North Carolina at Chapel Hill, March 1999. See http://www.cpc.unc.edu/projects/rlms/papers/Hlth1998.pdf (as of April 16, 2001).

Zohoori, Namvar, Thomas A. Mroz, Barry Popkin, Elena Glinskaya, Michael Lokshin, and Dominic Mancini, "Monitoring the Economic Transition in the Russian Federation and Its Implications for the Demographic Crisis—The Russian Longitudinal Monitoring Survey," *World Development,* Vol. 26, No. 11, November 1998, pp. 1977–1993.

Zuger, Abigail, "Freedom's Toll—Infectious Diseases Rising Again in Russia," *New York Times,* December 5, 2000.

Rand
1700 Main Street
Santa Monica, CA 90407-2138
Telephone: (310) 393-0411

INVOICE #: 229850

INV DATE: 5 APR 04

ACCOUNT #:62630

SOLD TO DR BEL CAMPBELL
7440 KAY DRIVE
PORT TOBACCO MD 20677-3157

SHIP TO DR BEL CAMPBELL
7440 KAY DRIVE
PORT TOBACCO MD 20677-3157

SALES AREA: Ruth M

CUSTOMER PO:

SHIPPED VIA: Book Post

TERMS: Gratis

ISBN	ORD	TITLE	PRICE	DIS	AMOUNT
0833029304	1	DIRE DEMOGRAPHICS POPULAT MR-1273$	.00	% $	Free

		SUB-TOTAL	$ .00
Main		SHIPPING	
		LESS PAYMENT	$
QUAN:	1		-----------
WEIGHT:	.38#	INVOICE TOTAL	$